Choices for the 21st Century

Defining Our Role in a Changing World

A Discussion Series on America's Future

5th Edition

CATALOGUING-IN-PUBLICATION DATA

Defining Our Role in a Changing World: A Discussion Series on
    America's Future: library reader / produced by the Choices for
    the 21st Century Education Project, Thomas J. Watson Jr. Institute
    for International Studies, Brown University.

    Providence, RI : Choices for the 21st Century Education Project,
        Thomas J. Watson Jr. Institute for International Studies, Brown
        University, c1998.

    VIII, 183 pp. : ill. ; 24 cm.

    1.   United States—Foreign relations—20th century.
  2.   United States—Politics and government—20th century.
  I.   Choices for the 21st Century Education Project.
  II. Defining Our Role in a Changing World.

ISBN 1-891306-00-6   327.73

CONTENTS

ACKNOWLEDGMENTS

This reader relies on the cooperation and expertise of a broad group of specialists with an inclusive range of political and disciplinary perspectives on each issue covered. We wish to express special thanks to the following researchers, academics, and policymakers for their assistance in the development and review of the materials included in this reader.

Kamal Abdel-Malek, Assistant Professor of Comparative Literature, Brown University

Engin D. Akarli, Professor of History, Brown University

Mark Anderson, Director, AFL-CIO Task Force on Trade

Susan Aronson, Professor of Economic History, George Washington University

Thomas Biersteker, Director, Watson Institute, Brown University

George Borts, Professor of Economics, Brown University

Jeffrey Boutwell, Associate Executive Officer, American Academy of Arts and Sciences

Robert Chen, Former Assistant Professor, World Hunger Program, Watson Institute, Brown University

Jarat Chopra, Research Associate, Watson Institute, Brown University

Elinor Despalatovic, Professor of History, Connecticut College

Sue Eckert, International Trade Consultant

Corinna-Barbara Francis, Former Faculty Fellow of Political Science, Brown University

Hilary French, Senior Researcher, Worldwatch Institute

C. Scipio Garling, Federation for American Immigration Reform

Mark Garrison, Senior Fellow, Watson Institute, Brown University

Theodore D. Goldfarb, Associate Professor of Chemistry, State University of New York at Stony Brook

Debbie Goldman, Research Economist, Communications Workers of America

Donald Greenburg, Associate Professor of Politics, Fairfield University

Jerome Grieder, Professor of History, Brown University

JoAnne Hart, Visiting Scholar, Political Science, Brown University

P. Terrence Hopmann, Director, Center for Foreign Policy Development, Watson Institute, Brown University

David C. Jacobson, Associate Professor of Judaic Studies, Brown University

Robert Kates, Former Director, World Hunger Program, Watson Institute, Brown University

Ying-Mao Kau, Professor of Political Science, Brown University

Amy T. LaPlante, American Immigration Lawyers Association

Robert Lee, Assistant Professor of American Civilization, Brown University

Mark Lindeman, Jacob K. Javits Fellow, Political Science, Columbia University

David McFadden, Associate Professor of History, Fairfield University

Linda B. Miller, Professor of Political Science, Wellesley College

Larry Minear, Co-Director, Humanitarianism and War Project, Watson Institute, Brown University

Eric Nordlinger, Former Professor of Political Science, Brown University

Eric Pallant, Visiting Assistant Professor, Center for Environmental Studies, Brown University

Marsha Pripstein Posusney, Assistant Professor of Political Science, Bryant College

Louis Putterman, Professor of Economics, Brown University

William Rose, Associate Professor of Political Science, Connecticut College

John Rouleau, Economic Planning Specialist

Stephen Shenfield, Research Associate, Watson Institute, Brown University

Richard Smoke, Research Director, Center for Foreign Policy Development, Watson Institute, Brown University

Peter Uvin, Associate Professor, World Hunger Program, Watson Institute, Brown University

Harold Ward, Director, Center for Environmental Studies, Brown University

Thomas Weiss, Research Director, Global Security Program, Watson Institute, Brown University

Michael White, Associate Professor of Sociology, Brown University

Albert Yee, Former Post-Doctoral Fellow, Watson Institute, Brown University

Alan Zuckerman, Professor of Political Science, Brown University

Many people contributed to the development of this reader. Mark Malkasian, curriculum developer for the Choices for the 21st Century Education Project, was the principal writer of much of the material from which this reader draws and was responsible for editing this edition of the reader. Mark Lindeman and William Rose co-authored a Choices college text, *The Role of the United States in a Changing World*. Karl Berger was the principal author of a Choices high school unit by the same name. Their contributions were critical to the development of the Futures framework used in this reader. The Choices Library Project began as a joint venture of the Choices Education Project and Options. We wish to express our appreciation to Marta Daniels, former director of Options, for her insightful contributions to earlier editions of this reader. Richard Gann of the Watson Institute assisted in the design of the reader. Fred Fullerton and Mary Lhowe, editors at the Watson Institute, provided editorial assistance. Previous editions of this reader were used in library discussions in Connecticut, Illinois, Indiana, Iowa, Maine, North Carolina, South Carolina, Utah, and Virginia. The feedback from discussion leaders and participants in these sessions has been most helpful to us as we worked on this fifth edition of the reader. Finally, we wish to thank the National Endowment for the Humanities for its continuing support to make the development and expansion of this program possible.

Susan Graseck, Director
Choices for the 21st Century Education Project

About the Program

Welcome to the *Choices for the 21st Century* program. This is a national, five-year old project organized by Brown University in collaboration with the National Endowment for the Humanities, state library systems, and state humanities councils.

Choices is a nationwide program designed to engage the American public in consideration of our nation's future in our rapidly changing world. It is a four-part, scholar-led reading and discussion series held in public libraries on the broad theme: "Who are we as a nation and how should we define our role in a changing world?"

The program does not advocate any particular point of view on this question. Rather, it seeks to bring citizens together in a non-partisan public space to deliberate about the direction in which the nation should head as the next century approaches. By learning together, listening respectfully to one another, weighing alternatives, and making difficult choices about competing values, it is hoped that we can work together toward a public voice on this all-encompassing public issue.

To ensure accurate and balanced material, the *Choices for the 21st Century* program takes care to incorporate the input of a broad group of academics and policymakers with an inclusive range of political and disciplinary perspectives, and submits all materials to rigorous review prior to publication. A full list of academics and policymakers who have served as consultants and reviewers of materials included in this reader can be found on pages iv-v.

This program is sponsored nationally by the Choices for the 21st Century Education Project of Brown University's Thomas J. Watson Jr. Institute for International Studies. Choices is an educational program that seeks to strengthen the quality of public life in the United States by encouraging the nation's schools and civic organizations to make the enrichment of public dialogue an integral part of their work.

The Choices Library Program is a partnership among the Choices national office, state library systems and state humanities councils, and local public libraries. The national office provides a reader for use in discussions, promotional materials for use by state and local coordinators, and on-site training for scholars and library staff who organize and lead the discussions in local libraries. The statewide partners provide organization and promotion on a statewide basis and work with the individual libraries that host the discussion series at the local level.

In addition to its work with library-based programs, Choices welcomes opportunities to assist a wide range of organizations to sponsor community-based public programs. Such programs may be organized in a range of formats from a series of four-to-ten discussions, to a college or extension course, to a single-day program.

Foreword

America was founded as a community of hope, a land of unlimited resources and endless possibilities. Our rights and freedoms, along with our responsibilities to each other, were established in the Declaration of Independence and the Virginia Statute for Religious Freedom. Written by Thomas Jefferson in 1779 and enacted in 1786, the Statute was the first document in the modern world to guarantee both freedom of belief and freedom of thought, cornerstones of civic participation and the American republic.

Freedom of belief and freedom of thought remain at the core of the continuing discussion, begun over 200 years ago, of what it means to be an American and what we want America to be. While we pledge allegiance to "one nation, under God, indivisible," to one nation with a shared past and a collective future, the truth is that America has always included a diversity of peoples, communities, and ideas. Such diversity has always spawned debate, and the myth of a unified community in agreement about what it wanted America to be in the 18th century is only a myth. The Virginia Statute itself was hotly contested, acrimoniously debated, and opposed by no less a revolutionary than Patrick Henry. Freedoms, rights, and responsibilities were never foregone conclusions. The founders, too, confronted difficult choices about what America was to be.

The freedoms debated and chosen 200 years ago remain at the cornerstone of *Choices for the 21st Century*. This program, in which you have chosen to participate, is based on the American tradition of public debate and the simple premise that everyday citizens determine the future of the nation and always have. Freedom demands civic participation, and public policy requires an educated and involved public. Freedom rests on the conviction that openness rather than certainty is the hallmark of the truly educated. Active engagement with other citizens and other ideas provides context and perspective to one's own beliefs. It challenges us to come together with neighbors; to confront differences; and to talk across age, race, gender, and religion in order to discover a shared future. The result is a "citizenry that is capable of confronting diversity, ambiguity, and conflict, overcoming prejudices and self-interest, enlarging its sympathies, tackling tough public issues, and envisioning possibilities beyond the limits of circumstance" (*The Humanities and the American Promise*).

By drawing on the highest ideals of America's democratic tradition — free and open debate, direct citizen participation, the pursuit of a shared vision that encompasses diverse viewpoints — *Choices for the 21st Century* is a superb means of achieving these goals. At the same time, it offers a rich array of opportunities for all participants to join in the creative work that Jefferson and his contemporaries began.

Robert C. Vaughan
President
Virginia Foundation for the
Humanities and Public Policy

Former Chair
Federation of State Humanities Councils

Chapter 1

The End of the Cold War: Challenges of a New Era

The vision of a free and diverse people in a democratic community evolved from the tradition of thought and experience that we call the humanities. Each generation must sustain and renew that vision through shared thought, study, inquiry, and discussion. Hence, study of the humanities is not only central to formal education but is also vital to daily life and work.

—*Federation of State Humanities Councils*

S ince the first days of the republic, Americans have debated how to balance our priorities at home with our relationships beyond our shores. In his farewell address of 1796, President George Washington warned Americans to "steer clear of permanent alliances with any portion of the foreign world." He particularly feared treaties that would entangle the United States in European disputes and inject the rivalries of the Old World into U.S. domestic politics. Yet Washington also recognized that the United States needed international trade in order to prosper. The first president advised his successors to follow a policy that would allow the United States to develop arrangements that were "temporary, and liable to be from time to time abandoned or varied, as experience and circumstances shall dictate; constantly keeping in view that 'tis folly in one nation to look for disinterested favors from another."

Over the past two centuries, the United States has changed beyond George Washington's imagining. Events have compelled Americans to re-think the U.S. role in the world on a number of occasions. Changes in the American scene — unmatched economic growth, ever-widening global power, waves of immigration, and startling social transformations — have inevitably left Americans wrestling with conflicting foreign policy ideas de-rived from various aspects of the American experience. Time and again, Americans have argued about what interests and values, if any, were at stake outside the country, and how the United States should respond.

Post-Cold War questions

For four decades following World War II, most Americans agreed that U.S. foreign policy should be grounded in three points of consensus: U.S. security needs were at the heart of our country's national interests; the Soviet Union was the principal threat to our security; and the United States had no choice but to be actively involved in international affairs. According to the logic of the Cold War, the United States was compelled to counter the Soviets in Afghanistan, Central America, Southern Africa, and other con-tested regions.

This broad agreement endured despite sharp disagreements over how far our commitment should extend. In the late 1960s, for instance, the Viet-nam War — increasingly controversial in itself — created intense economic pressures at a time when the United States was also fighting a federal "War on Poverty." Some observers believe that the nation's attempt to pursue both struggles condemned the United States to fail on each front. (Some argue that, in fact, neither "war" was winnable.) Despite these differences, high levels of defense spending and a global U.S. military presence were largely accepted by Americans as central to U.S. security.

Today, the United States finds itself again in a world that has fundamentally changed. The Soviet Union is gone (although its nuclear arsenal remains). No single adversary looms as a threat to U.S. interests, at least not for now. The United States is the world's sole superpower, with unrivaled military strength and international influence.

But this new international position brings with it new challenges. There is a growing recognition that the world of the 21st century will be an international world — a world in which communication is instant and universal, a world in which local economics encompass international trade relationships, and a world in which environmental and health concerns spill over political boundaries. It is also a world in transition. The emergence of China on the world stage, volatility in the Middle East, uncertainties in Russia, and a myriad of conflicts elsewhere remind us of the security dangers we all face in the nuclear age. Despite these growing concerns, Americans today seem oddly disengaged from the world beyond our shores.

There are periods of history when profound changes occur all of a sudden....We are now in one of those periods, which obliges the United States to rethink its role in the world, just as it was forced to do by the cataclysmic changes that followed the end of the Second World War.

—Stanley Hoffmann, professor of European studies, Harvard University

At home too, Americans are experiencing growing pains. While the economy is thriving, at least for the moment, long-term issues remain unanswered. The future of middle-class entitlements such as social security and medicare remain in question. The gulf between the haves and the have-nots continues to pull at our social fabric. Most Americans agree that our nation's civic life would benefit from an injection of commitment and purpose, but confusion about how and where to start presents a roadblock.

Debating a new definition of security

The collapse of the Soviet Union has meant that we no longer share common understandings about what the U.S. role in the world should be, or about how we should balance our foreign policy interests with our domestic responsibilities. Americans, both policymakers and the public, have been left to construct a new vision for our country. Central to this debate is the search for a common understanding of national security that can guide our foreign and domestic policies in the environment of the post-Cold War world.

National security has generally been thought of as falling within the domain of America's military and diplomatic corps. At the most fundamental level, our country's security establishment is responsible for protecting the United States from outside attack. During the Cold War, that meant countering the armed might of the Soviet Union. Over the past decades, but with particular urgency in the last five years, some Americans have argued forcefully that the United States must abandon its narrow definition of national security. According to this argument, the country placed too much emphasis during the Cold War on countering external military threats, while it neglected vital economic and social goals. We need, it is said, a new vision of security that embraces better conditions at home, economic competitiveness abroad, and a more coherent response to global problems such as environmental degradation and other key concerns.

> *A successful foreign policy requires an intellectual underpinning or mooring in a vision of the country's mission in the world. The lesson from Bosnia is that this is not merely an academic exercise but an important practical necessity.*
> —Jonathan Clarke, British diplomat

While there is plenty of room for disagreement about what constitutes security today, there are some things on which most Americans can agree. Just about everyone agrees that the United States should remain independent and as safe as possible from outside attack. Just about everyone also agrees that national independence and safety are not enough. America should be a good place to live — a place where hard work is rewarded, where quality education is accessible to all, where health care services meet our medical needs, and where we and our children are safe from crime. And just about everyone agrees, at least in the abstract, that it would be desirable for all countries to treat their citizens well, and for all countries to work together in order to solve our common problems. Some people would call all of these things aspects of

> *How involved America should be in world politics and what values it should seek to foster — and at what cost and risk — are questions that remain open, unanswered, and largely unaddressed.*
> —Robert Jervis, professor of political science
> Columbia University

"security." Others would not. But just about everyone would like to see them happen. Where Americans disagree is on the extent to which each of these broad goals might be possible, and above all on what costs, risks, and trade-offs the country should accept in setting its priorities among them.

These are significant disagreements, sometimes requiring painful choices. We may want to equip the U.S. military with state-of-the-art weaponry, but what toll will this exact on the economy, and are we willing to pay it? We may want to promote and defend democracy abroad, but what will we say if American soldiers are killed, or if our government must spend less on domestic programs in order to pay for our overseas involvement? We may want to focus on our domestic problems, but what if the countries of the world start closing their markets to us, or if Europe spirals toward war? We may want to cooperate more closely with other countries, but what if their policy preferences clash sharply with those of the United States, or if their indecisiveness prevents our country from acting when its interests and duties are clear? We may want cheap imports and high wages, but what if these goals seem to lead in opposite directions? We may want all of these things. What trade-offs are we willing to accept?

Public choices

These are difficult issues that engage and often perplex our minds and our hearts. If clear thinking alone could settle them, then perhaps national policy could be left to the experts. But the experts disagree as sharply and as passionately on these issues as the public does. This is a historic moment, a time when U.S. leaders are struggling to set the nation's public policy agenda for the post-Cold War era. It is a time when input from concerned citizens is more important than ever.

The subject of this series can ultimately be reduced to one central question: "How should we define our role in a changing world?" To address this question, we must not only consider the changes taking place

---

What are Public Choices?

Public deliberation is at the heart of a healthy democracy. The kinds of decisions that citizens can and must make — "public choices" — are distinctly different from the sort that most policy experts consider.

•Public choices address the goals and purposes toward which we want the nation's policy to aim.

•Public choices are grounded in value judgments; "expert choices" reflect technical considerations.

•Public choices consider long-term policy directions, not short-term strategies for implementation.

in the world around us, but we must also consider the diverse but shared values that have driven policy decisions since our nation's beginnings, values that together define our American political culture.

This *Choices for the 21st Century* program is different from most discussion series with which you may be familiar. It is more than an intellectual exercise intended to help you understand what the experts and policymakers are thinking and doing. Experts can clarify the goals and trade-offs the nation must consider and they can lay out specific policy choices, along with their costs and risks. But experts and policymakers have no special insight into which goals should have priority and which risks are worth taking. These are decisions that all Americans must make together. It is time for a national conversation about America's future.

At the heart of this series is a "choices" framework of four alternative visions, or Futures, for the next decade. These are not the only possible Futures, but together they represent a balanced spectrum of views and serve as vehicles for raising important issues. The Futures are intentionally framed in very stark terms. Each reflects very different assumptions about the goals of U.S. foreign policy, the nature of international relations, and the place of foreign policy in our national life. They are offered as a tool to help you weigh the pros and cons, risks and trade-offs of a range of fundamentally different alternatives and to consider the values that guide each alternative. In the end, you will be asked to draw from your understanding of these Futures to decide for yourself what you think U.S. policy should be in the years ahead.

What We Ask of You

•*Listen respectfully to the views of others and understand why they take the positions that they do.*

•*Consider the history of the issue under discussion.*

•*Weigh pros and cons, risks and trade-offs of alternative policies.*

•*Come to your own judgment based on serious consideration of divergent views.*

•*Search for the common ground on which to move forward at this critical moment in our nation's history.*

A guide to your reader

Your reader has nine chapters. In this chapter, you have read about the currents of thought that have run through American history and explored how recent changes in the international environment have raised new questions for U.S. policy. The first session in your discussion series will be devoted to understanding the four Futures or visions for America. The Futures are described in chapter 2.

In the middle sessions, you will examine specific challenges facing the United States today. Your reader includes six topics: "The Search for Peace in an Age of Conflict: Debating the U.S. Role," "Global Environmental Problems: Implications for U.S. Policy," "U.S. Trade Policy: Competing in a Global Economy," "China on the World Stage: Weighing the U.S. Response," "Shifting Sands: Balancing U.S. Interests in the Middle East," and "U.S. Immigration Policy in an Unsettled World." Two will be selected for discussion. We encourage you to browse through the others.

The challenge topics are intended to give you an opportunity to consider the direction of U.S. policy in today's world. Together, the six topics illustrate the transformation of international relations since the end of the Cold War. Only a decade ago, discussion of global warming was largely limited to scientific panels, while the North American Free Trade Agreement (NAFTA) and the mushrooming of international peacekeeping operations had yet to appear on the foreign policy agenda. In addition, the challenge topics point to the increasing overlap between domestic and foreign affairs. As events have shown, U.S. immigration policy cannot be separated from the international refugee crisis or U.S.-Mexican relations. Global environmental problems threaten the entire planet, but are rooted in local and national decisions about industrial production and regulation, forest policy, and much more.

Democracy is not something we have — it is something we do.
—Frances Moore Lappe, co-director
Institute for the Arts of Democracy

Finally, chapter 9 provides background for the concluding session of your series. In this session, you will be called upon to develop your own preferred Future Five, a Future that describes the role you believe America should play in the years ahead.

The primary goal of this program is to enhance public deliberation on the future of U.S. policy in our rapidly changing world and to increase public participation in the democratic process. Over the course of this series, you will have the opportunity to challenge your own thinking in the company of others. You will want to ask yourself what has surprised you most about your own thinking regarding the best course for America's future. Has understanding the views of others influenced how you view the question? What is most important to you? Often the things we care deeply about are in conflict. What consequences are unacceptable? What trade-offs are you willing to make? Are there grounds for agreement among the participants in your group?

Before you leave the final session of this series, we ask that you complete the brief ballot found at the end of this book. The results of this ballot will be tabulated and analyzed and then distributed to elected officials in your state and in Washington. This is your opportunity to add your voice to the ongoing national conversation.

Chapter 2

Considering Four Futures

A Word about the Futures

The central question of this series is, "Who are we as a nation, and where are we going?" There are ultimately no simple answers. The program uses a framework of alternative "Futures" as a tool to help you think about this important question. The Futures highlight contrasting policy directions. Each is driven by a very different set of values reflecting different assumptions about the goals of U.S. foreign policy, the nature of international relations, and the place of foreign policy in our national life. In stark terms, the Futures illustrate some fundamentally different paths, each with distinctive pros and cons, risks and trade-offs.

These Futures are not the only choices on this issue. During the final session of this discussion series, you will have an opportunity to define a Future of your own reflecting your judgment about the role that you believe the United States should play in the post-Cold War world.

Futures in Brief

FUTURE 1 — STANDING UP FOR DEMOCRACY AND HUMAN RIGHTS

As the home of freedom and democracy, the United States has a special responsibility to promote American ideals throughout the world. History is on our side, but we must lend the process of change a helping hand. We must act boldly to stop the world's bullies and elevate the international standard for human rights. The United States must uphold a principled foreign policy. Without the Soviet threat hanging over us, Americans can make human rights and democracy our top foreign policy priority. By standing up for American values, we have the power to make the world a safer and more humane place for everyone.

FUTURE 2 — CHARTING A STABLE COURSE

In a world that has grown dangerously unstable, U.S. foreign policy must strive for order and security. To navigate through these unpredictable times, the United States cannot be distracted by crusading idealists or short-sighted isolationists. We have to concentrate on issues that are of vital importance to U.S. interests. Our relations with individual countries should serve our economic and security needs. Americans have no choice but to accept the world as it is, and do our best to make our country stronger.

FUTURE 3 — BUILDING A MORE COOPERATIVE WORLD

We live in an interdependent and interconnected world. In an age when new breakthroughs in communication and transportation are making our planet smaller, we cannot separate U.S. problems from the problems affecting the world as a whole. We must take the initiative to bring the nations of the world together in a spirit of cooperation. The United Nations should be granted more responsibility to deal with environmental pollution, refugees, AIDS, and other global problems. We must recognize that our fate as Americans is bound together with the fate of all of humanity.

FUTURE 4 — TURNING INWARD

Since the late 1940s, the United States has spent billions of dollars a year defending our allies in Western Europe and East Asia. We have distributed billions more in foreign aid to countries throughout the developing world. Enough is enough. Americans simply cannot afford to be the world's generous uncle. Instead, we have to turn inward and deal with the real threats facing Americans. We must sharply scale back our foreign involvement. U.S. troops overseas should be brought home and military spending cut in half. Let the rest of the world learn to fend for itself. Americans have to put their own needs first.

FUTURE 1

Standing up for democracy and human rights

As the home of freedom and democracy, the United States has a special responsibility to promote American ideals throughout the world. In the Soviet Union, we saw how the values we hold dear inspired ordinary people to challenge the communist system. In many other countries as well, democracy and human rights have made important inroads in recent years. History is on our side, but we must lend the process of change a helping hand. Many states remain in the hands of cruel and undemocratic leaders who terrorize their own people and threaten their neighbors. We must act boldly to stop the world's bullies and elevate the international standard for human rights.

The United States must uphold a principled foreign policy. Without the Soviet threat hanging over us, Americans can make human rights and democracy our top foreign policy priority. We should support countries that are taking their first steps toward democracy. Foreign aid should be provided to governments that respect human rights and tolerate diversity within their societies. At times, we may have to act on our own and use military force to defend our principles in the international arena. However, once the United States clearly demonstrates its commitment to democracy and human rights, few will dare test our country's resolve.

> Today, the greatest danger to America is not some foreign enemy; it is the possibility that we will...allow the momentum toward democracy to stall...and forget what the history of this century reminds us: that problems, if left unattended, will all too often come home to haunt America.
>
> —Madeleine Albright, secretary of state

By standing up for American values, we have the power to make the world a safer and more humane place for everyone.

What do we have to do?

• We should craft U.S. foreign policy around the principles of democracy and human rights. The United States should not tolerate international aggression and flagrant abuses of human rights from regional trouble-makers, such as the leaders of Iraq, North Korea, and Cuba. We should pressure China to allow its own citizens more freedom and to recognize the rights of the Tibetan people. We should promote democracy in the former Soviet bloc. We should pressure Turkey, Saudi Arabia, Indonesia, and other long-time allies to improve their human rights record as well.

•**Militarily**, we should use our country's might to defend the principles of democracy and human rights. We should keep our troops deployed around the world to prevent aggressive dictators from taking over their weaker neighbors. U.S. forces should also step in, as they did in Haiti, to stop tyrants from brutally repressing people within their own borders. We should break our alliances with governments that do not value democracy and human rights. This may mean closing our military bases in countries like Saudi Arabia and Turkey. In addition, we should permit arms exports only to our democratic allies.

In an increasingly interdependent world Americans have a growing stake in how other countries govern, or misgovern, themselves. The larger and more close-knit the community of nations that choose democratic forms of government, the safer and more prosperous Americans will be.

—Strobe Talbott, deputy secretary of state

•**Economically**, we should impose trade boycotts and sanctions on countries that grossly violate the human rights of their citizens. We should use the promise of trade benefits and economic aid to encourage the countries of the former Soviet bloc and the developing world to adopt democratic principles and respect human rights.

Costs: This Future will require that we double our foreign aid budget (which currently accounts for less than 1 percent of total government spending). Our military forces would also be protected from further budget cuts, with more emphasis on strengthening our rapid deployment forces. Meanwhile, U.S. trade with undemocratic nations may suffer. For example, weapons exports to Saudi Arabia would be blocked unless the government there changes its policies. As the most dangerous regimes are replaced by democratic governments, we can expect military threats to gradually fade and global trade to increase.

Future 1 is based on these beliefs

•The United States is respected throughout the world as the champion of freedom, justice, democracy, and tolerance. As Americans, we have a special responsibility to promote democracy and respect for human rights around the world, even if we have to act alone.

• Tyrannical regimes are the main human cause of suffering in the world. Without the checks and balances of democracy to restrain them, dictators typically oppress their own people, fan the flames of aggressive nationalism, and threaten their neighbors. To support them or turn a blind eye to their aggression is dangerous and immoral. We must stop them now.

• We have the most powerful military in the world and should not be afraid to use it to make the world a better place. As long as we remain militarily on guard, we can expect fewer and fewer problems from the world's troublemakers, and we may take bolder steps than ever before to promote democracy and respect for human rights.

Critics say:

1. Pressuring other governments to change their ways will spark international criticism that the United States is pursuing a double standard, particularly in light of the poverty and racial problems here at home.

2. Stressing the division between democratic and undemocratic countries will split the world into two opposing camps, as in the Cold War. Valuable allies, such as Saudi Arabia, will be lost while emerging powers in the developing world, such as China, will be branded as enemies.

3. Refusing to trade with undemocratic countries will only hurt the U.S. economy, since most of our trading partners will continue to do business with these nations. Meanwhile, the United States will cut itself off from important sources of oil and other raw materials.

4. Many societies in the developing world and the former Soviet bloc reject our definition of democracy and human rights. In the Islamic countries of the Middle East, for example, most people value their traditional way of life and may not want American-style freedoms. In addition, events in Russia have shown that U.S. foreign aid and goodwill can do little to alter deep-seated forces of history and culture.

Supporters say:

1. As recent events in Bosnia and Haiti have shown, aggressive tyrants will back down only when the United States steps into a crisis and acts decisively.

2. Since democracies are much less likely to start wars against other democracies, we will be making the world a more peaceful place in the long run.

3. If we wait until the world's bullies become so powerful that we must confront them, as we did with Hitler in World War II, the cost will be enormous.

4. As new democracies take root and their economies prosper, they will become strong trading partners for the United States.

FUTURE 2 ━━━━━━━━━━━━━━━━━━━━━━

Charting a stable course

In a world that has grown dangerously unstable, U.S. foreign policy must strive for order and security. Angry nationalism in Russia, rising poverty and chaos in the developing world, the pressures of global economic competition, and other threats have created an international minefield for U.S. leaders. To navigate through these unpredictable times, the United States cannot be distracted by crusading idealists or short-sighted isolationists. A level-headed, calculating perspective is required. We have to concentrate on issues that are of vital importance to U.S. interests. That

> *America must be selective in its actions. It cannot take on all the world's troubles. The public will soon grow weary if this country takes on the role of world policeman, or world nanny, or international Don Quixote.*
>
> —*James Schlesinger, former defense secretary*

means focusing our energies on protecting our key trade relationships and stopping the spread of nuclear weapons to unfriendly nations. In volatile regions, like the Middle East, we should use our influence to establish a stable balance of power.

First and foremost, U.S. foreign policy must promote U.S. interests. Our relations with individual countries should serve our economic and security needs, not seek to change the world. In this competitive world, the United States cannot afford to sacrifice important trade ties to advance dreamy political ideals. Neither should we give up our influence in international affairs for the sake of global cooperation. Americans have no choice but to accept the world as it is, and do our best to make our country stronger.

What do we have to do?

• We should remain actively involved in international affairs. Our military alliances and trading partnerships with Western Europe and Japan should continue to serve as the foundation of global stability. We should also seek to influence the other great powers of the world, particularly Russia and China. In areas of conflict, such as the Balkans

We do not have the luxury of putting our leadership on hold until we get our domestic house in order. Unfortunately, there is no holiday from history.
—Brent Scowcroft,
former national security adviser

and the Caribbean, the United States should be willing to act alone, when necessary, to protect U.S. interests. We should act decisively to prevent countries like North Korea and Iran from acquiring nuclear weapons or sponsoring international terrorism.

• **Militarily**, we should maintain a strong presence abroad. Through our continued commitment to the North Atlantic Treaty Organization (NATO), we should guard against attempts by Russia to restore its empire by force. Russian politicians with an appetite for expansion must be shown that we will defend our interests in the former Soviet bloc. Likewise, U.S. military ties to Japan, South Korea, and other East Asian countries should serve to keep Chinese ambitions in check. Military aid and arms exports should also be used as a tool of U.S. foreign policy. For example, we should assist rebel groups that are fighting to overthrow anti-American regimes. U.S. troops should be sent into battle only to protect vital U.S. interests, as was the case when the United States and its allies drove Iraq out of the oil-rich country of Kuwait. Finally, U.S. forces should serve as international peacekeepers in a conflict area only after the fighting has ended.

• **Economically**, we should not let political differences with other countries harm our important trade relationships. We should not pressure other countries to change their domestic policies as long as they do not oppose U.S. interests. Economic aid should be used to advance U.S. trade and investment in the former Soviet bloc and the developing world.

Costs: This Future will require us to maintain high levels of military spending to remain the world's superpower. If other nations reduce their military spending, we may in turn be able to cut our defense budget.

Future 2 is based on these beliefs

•The United States, like most other countries, benefits from stability. Efforts to fundamentally change the international system inevitably backfire, resulting in dangerous instability and increased suffering.

•In our violent and competitive world, international stability and security depends largely on the United States. More than any other country, the United States has the power to keep power-hungry nations in check and bring stability to volatile regions.

•We must be practical and maintain friendly relations with stable but undemocratic governments, such as Saudi Arabia and China, in order to protect U.S. interests.

Critics say:

1. Maintaining our alliances with cruel dictators sets back the cause of human rights and the worldwide movement toward democracy.

2. Preoccupying ourselves with containing the influence of China and Russia will undermine international cooperation on critical global issues, such as controlling nuclear weapons and cleaning up pollution.

3. Staying out of conflicts until the fighting has ended will meaning turning our back on future incidents of genocide and "ethnic cleansing," as was the case in Rwanda and Bosnia.

4. Trying to play one country off another is a reckless game. If we and other nations had not armed Iraq in the 1980s to keep its neighbor, Iran, in check, we would not have had to fight Iraq in the Persian Gulf War. As World War I showed, balance-of-power schemes eventually collapse like a house of cards.

Supporters say:

1. U.S. involvement in areas of tension, such as the Middle East and the Korean peninsula, will contribute to a stable balance of power and reduce the possibility of war. As a result, countries will be less likely to seek to acquire nuclear, biological, and chemical weapons.

2. A forceful U.S. presence in international affairs will discourage emerging powers, such as China, from building up their military might and expanding their influence at the expense of their neighbors.

3. Maintaining our long-standing military alliances in Western Europe and East Asia will help protect U.S. interests and put today's shaky international system on firm ground.

4. By keeping politics from interfering with our business interests, the United States will gain new markets for our products and enjoy access to the raw materials critical to our economic prosperity.

FUTURE 3 ——————————————————————————

Building a more cooperative world

We live in an interdependent and interconnected world. Environmental problems, such as global warming, threaten the ecology of the entire planet. Political upheaval in the Caribbean and the former Soviet bloc sends waves of refugees to U.S. shores. National boundaries do little to halt the spread of AIDS, international drug trafficking, terrorism, and other global scourges. In an age when new breakthroughs in communication and transportation are making our planet smaller, we cannot separate U.S. problems from the problems affecting the world as a whole.

We must take the initiative to bring the nations of the world together in a spirit of cooperation. The United Nations (UN) should be granted more responsibility to deal with environmental pollution, refugees, AIDS, and

> *The post-Cold War era...provides...the opportunity to strive for truly collective security and an international rule of law, in which self-help by the use of military force for resolving conflicts among nations loses its legitimacy.*
> —*Carl Kaysen, Robert McNamara,*
>   *George Rathjens*

other global problems. As the world's most powerful country, we must be willing to relinquish a portion of our sovereignty to the UN. In addition, the United States should join with Japan, Western Europe, and other wealthy allies to help the countries of Asia, Africa, and Latin America lift themselves out of poverty. Instead of trying to police the world ourselves, we should use military force outside of North America only under UN leadership. Building a more cooperative world will not be easy. Americans will have to reassess their national interests. In the end, however, we must recognize that our fate as Americans is bound together with the fate of all of humanity. On our shrinking planet, there is nowhere to hide from the global challenges of the future.

What do we have to do?

•We should consult with other nations as we chart our foreign policy. Whenever possible, we should act not on our own but as part of a coordinated international effort. We should increase our financial support for the UN and contribute to UN efforts to maintain global peace, address humanitarian crises, and enforce sanctions against countries that violate the standards of the international community.

•**Militarily**, we should not send our troops to fight outside of North America without the approval of the fifteen-nation UN Security Council. (As permanent members on the council, the United States, Britain, France, Russia, and China each have veto power over the council's decisions.) We should work to establish a permanent UN military force ready to bring peace to troubled areas. At the same time, we should gradually reduce the number of U.S. troops around the world, with the goal of eventually having no independent U.S. forces outside of North America. Finally, the United States should lead a worldwide effort to reduce arms exports and lower military spending.

•**Economically**, we should spearhead international efforts to improve economic and environmental conditions in the developing world and the former Soviet bloc. In exchange for cooperation on environmental issues, we should forgive the billions of dollars in debt that are owed us by countries in the developing world and the former Soviet bloc. In accordance with UN recommendations, we should earmark 0.7 percent of our gross national product (about $48 billion in 1995) for economic assistance. These funds will be administered primarily by international organizations. Rather than using aid to pursue short-term foreign policy gains, we should join in an international effort to reduce poverty and lay the foundation for greater global harmony.

Costs: As a permanent UN military force becomes established, we will no longer need to remain the world's military superpower, and will be able to sharply reduce our defense spending. Most of the money saved will be earmarked for economic assistance projects in the developing world and the former Soviet bloc, and for arming and funding our share of the UN force.

Future 3 is based on these beliefs

• We live in an interdependent world. If humanity is to have a hopeful future, we must work cooperatively to address global problems that affect us all, such as the destruction of tropical rain forests, refugee crises driven by conflict, and nuclear proliferation.

• U.S. problems are global problems, and can be solved only through global cooperation. Trying to deal with ozone depletion, AIDS, and other global problems without the involvement of all nations is like building a dam halfway across a raging river.

A pragmatic vision of the post-Cold War world involves multiple international organizations dedicated to solving particular problems. These would have overlapping membership and substantial power for well-defined purposes. The United States would make cooperative problem solving a central theme of its diplomatic efforts.
—Alice Rivlin, director
Office of Management and Budget

• Cooperating globally is only fair. The earth does not belong to us. Americans comprise only 5 percent of the world's population, and the United States is but one of nearly 200 countries in the world. Neither the United States nor any other country has the right to decide on its own to pressure another country to behave in a certain way.

Critics say:

1. By handing over so much of our power to international organizations, we will lose much of our international influence. China, Russia, Japan, and other leading powers will take advantage of our cooperative spirit to make themselves stronger at our expense.

2. Giving up our option to use force outside of North America will severely limit U.S. flexibility internationally and encourage our enemies to defy us.

3. Many countries are run by corrupt and cruel governments. Strengthening international organizations in which thieves and tyrants have a voice and giving them more foreign aid will only make such regimes stronger.

4. Spending billions of dollars trying to solve the world's ills will deprive us of the resources we need to address the many problems we face at home.

Supporters say:

1. The world is becoming increasingly interdependent. Global problems are posing an ever greater challenge to the nations of the world and usually do not lend themselves to military solutions. Cooperating globally puts us in step with the world of the future.

2. Giving more power and authority to international organizations does not make us powerless. On the contrary, individual nations are already powerless to cope with a growing range of global problems. By bringing nations together to solve common problems, we will gain the strength to deal with the challenges of tomorrow's world.

3. The economic assistance we gave Western Europe and Japan after World War II helped boost international trade and strengthen the U.S. economy. Aiding the countries of the developing world and the former Soviet bloc will likewise benefit the United States in the long run.

4. Strengthening the UN and other international institutions will help firmly anchor China, Russia, and other unpredictable powers in an international order characterized by cooperation and responsible behavior.

FUTURE 4

Turning inward

Since the late 1940s, the United States has spent billions of dollars a year defending our allies in Western Europe and East Asia. We have distributed billions more in foreign aid to countries throughout the developing world. Economically, we have stood for the principles of free trade, and have opened the American market to exports from countries that follow unfair trade practices. And what do we have to show for our efforts? Our so-called allies, such as Japan and Germany, took advantage of the defense umbrella we offered to pull ahead of us economically in many areas. Much of the foreign aid we have given has been squandered on ungrateful Third World tyrants. Finally, our economic competitors have exploited our commitment to free trade to saddle us with chronic trade deficits. Enough is enough. Americans simply cannot afford to be the world's generous uncle. Instead, we have to turn inward and deal with the real threats facing Americans: our struggle for economic competitiveness, spiraling national debt, decaying inner cities, declining educational standards, a shaky health care system, crime, drugs, AIDS, and homelessness. If we do not straighten out our priorities, we will become a second-rate nation.

We must sharply scale back our foreign involvement. U.S. troops overseas should be brought home and military spending cut in half. We will still have plenty of military muscle to defend North America and protect Americans abroad, but we should no longer sacrifice our future to maintain our status as a military superpower. Foreign aid, other than for humanitarian emergencies, should be eliminated. The hundreds of billions of dollars we save should be used to address pressing national problems and reduce taxes. Let the rest of the world learn to fend for itself. As Americans, we have to put our own needs first.

> *What is desperately required is a psychological turn inward....Taking on new commitments in the Middle East and Persian Gulf while maintaining most of the old ones in Europe and the Far East cannot be justified in the face of a disastrous domestic agenda...*
>
> —William G. Hyland, former editor
>   Foreign Affairs

What do we have to do?

• We should cut our military and political ties overseas and refocus our attention on domestic problems. Our attitude toward other countries should not be belligerent or hostile, but the world should understand that the United States must put the interests of Americans first.

• **Militarily**, we should gradually phase out our alliances outside of North America. We should make it clear that we will join other countries militarily only when our security is directly threatened. We should redesign our armed forces to defend only North America. A small force should be specially trained to respond around the world when American lives are at stake (for example, during a hostage crisis, or to evacuate Americans from a hostile country). These steps will allow the United States to gradually cut its military budget in half.

It is primarily by example, never by precept, that a country such as ours exerts the most useful influence beyond its borders....unless we preserve the quality, the vigor and the morale of our own society, we will be of little use to anyone at all.
—George F. Kennan, former ambassador to the Soviet Union

• **Economically**, we should protect American industries from unfair foreign competition. U.S. trade policy should be driven strictly by American economic interests, not by idealistic foreign policy goals to promote global harmony or bolster democracy. The United States should withdraw from the North American Free Trade Agreement (NAFTA) with Mexico and Canada, and give up efforts to prop up the Mexican economy. We should work to substantially reduce our dependence on foreign oil. As we scale down our military, we should rely more on trade boycotts, sanctions, and other non-military levers of influence as our main tools to make the United States secure.

Costs: This Future will allow us to cut our military budget in half, which will eventually free up nearly $135 billion annually. We will redirect this money toward addressing our domestic problems and reducing taxes.

Future 4 is based on these beliefs

• The greatest threats facing the United States today are at home. To remain strong as a nation, we must turn our energies away from foreign affairs and face these threats.

• Most of the problems afflicting the world beyond U.S. borders cannot be solved by the United States. Rather, U.S. leaders should strive to ensure that the misery and poverty common to most of the planet do not overtake the United States.

• International power and influence in today's world are measured in terms of economic strength, not military might. In the global struggle for economic competitiveness, the United States cannot afford to fall behind its economic rivals in East Asia and Western Europe. In this contest, the military and foreign entanglements that the United States built up during the Cold War are a burden on our country.

Critics say:

1. Pulling our troops out of Western Europe, the Middle East, and East Asia will upset the worldwide balance of power and spark wars. In response, insecure countries will seek to acquire nuclear, biological, and chemical weapons.

2. Deeply cutting our military power will leave the United States incapable of standing up for democracy or protecting our economic interests. As in World War II, the United States will eventually be forced to undertake a costly military build-up to combat threats from overseas.

3. After winning the Cold War, we would be foolish to abandon our long-standing goals of promoting democracy and human rights internationally, especially in China and other emerging powers. We cannot retreat from our position of international leadership if we want to help create a better world in the 21st century.

4. The Persian Gulf War showed us that economic sanctions have their limits, and that military strength is still a decisive factor in shaping the world. If we sharply cut our military spending, we will be unable to defeat the next Saddam Hussein that crosses us.

Supporters say:

1. Eliminating costly and ill-conceived foreign policy ventures — such as promoting democracy in Russia or lifting Mexico out of poverty — will free up resources needed to restore American economic strength.

2. It is time to reap the fruits of our victory in the Cold War. Now that there are no major military threats facing us or any of our allies, we can afford to beat most of our swords into plowshares.

3. By giving top priority to our domestic problems, we will be in a much better position to serve as a model for other countries.

4. Sharply cutting U.S. military spending will encourage other leading powers to reduce their spending on defense and will lower tensions worldwide.

Chapter 3

The Search for Peace in an Age of Conflict: Debating the U.S. Role

In a rugged corner of northwestern Bosnia, a unit of American soldiers in the fall of 1996 found itself caught in the middle of Europe's bloodiest conflict since World War II. On one side were hundreds of Bosnian Muslim refugees demanding to return to their abandoned homes a few miles away. A few threw stones or hurled insults at the Americans and Russians blocking their way. On the other side were Bosnian Serb policemen eager for a fight. They openly defied American requests to allow the refugees safe passage and instead fired on the handful of young men that slipped past barriers of razor wire. The point of contention was a remote village that had been reduced to rubble during three and one-half years of war.

By most accounts, it was an odd place for the world's only remaining superpower. With all of America's might, the U.S. peacekeepers were largely powerless to resolve Bosnia's deep-rooted problems. At the same time, the peacekeeping mission in Bosnia had achieved a measure of success for both U.S. foreign policy and the cause of international peace. The United States had played a decisive role in stopping a war that had claimed more than 200,000 lives. America's commitment of 20,000 peacekeeping troops had helped cement a shaky peace agreement in December 1995 and prevented the renewal of fighting.

Americans were justifiably torn by the U.S. position in Bosnia. Few had been familiar with Bosnia's troubled history before U.S. diplomats and troops became involved in the country. Fewer still saw Bosnia as an area of vital U.S. interests. Nonetheless, the American public was genuinely moved by the suffering and injustice of the conflict. As the war dragged on, pressure mounted on President Bill Clinton to take action.

The issues raised by Bosnia touch directly on our country's role in the world. Without the menace of Soviet communism at the top of the U.S. international agenda, conflicts in places like Bosnia have captured the foreign policy spotlight. And yet Bosnia does not fit into the Cold War parameters of national security.

The fledgling state does not have vital natural resources, like the oil of the Persian Gulf region. Nor is there concern that the Balkans are a breeding ground for communism or another potent ideology that would present a worldwide threat to U.S. interests. Moreover, the region is unlikely to give rise to a power-hungry dictator comparable to Adolf Hitler. Rather, Bosnia represents a new set of challenges for Americans.

The conflicts that have arisen since the end of the Cold War have compelled us to rethink our national interests and our relationship with the international community. Before our country decides whether or not to send American troops to trouble spots abroad, we must grapple with a wide range of difficult questions.

Defining Terms

State sovereignty

Sovereignty means freedom from external control. Traditionally, governments have strongly defended the principle of sovereignty. They have worked cooperatively only with the understanding that their sovereignty would be protected. In practical terms, sovereignty has never been absolute. Strong countries influence the policies of weaker countries. In recent decades, sovereign states have encountered pressure from institutions that extend beyond national boundaries as well as from minority groups or regional interests within their borders.

Territorial integrity

Territorial integrity means that national borders should not be forcibly changed. Since the end of World War II, the international community has upheld the principle of territorial integrity as a means of maintaining peace and stability. Although statesmen argue that support for territorial integrity has discouraged aggression and prevented the breakup of states, the principle of territorial integrity has also left much of Africa and Asia with borders drawn by 19th century colonial powers. Africa, in particular, has been torn by conflicts that often trace their origins to inherited colonial borders.

Self-determination

Self-determination means the right of a people to govern its own affairs. Self-determination often conflicts with the principles of state sovereignty and territorial integrity. With literally thousands of ethnic groups in the world, fully honoring the principle of self-determination could lead to the creation of thousands of countries.

Minority rights

Minority rights means establishing a special set of laws to protect minority groups. Minority rights may allow a group to operate its own schools, promote its language and culture, or take responsibility for the functions of local government. In many parts of the world, central governments have refused to concede rights to minority groups. They fear that granting minority rights will encourage minority groups to form separate states. Others believe that granting minority communities local autonomy and group rights will prevent conflict.

Conflict resolution

Conflict resolution means the involvement of an outside party to bring peace to an area. Approaches to conflict resolution generally fall into three categories: diplomacy in which an outside party may arrange negotiations or offer itself as an arbitrator, sanctions intended to pressure a party to change its policies, and the threat or use of force. ❏

How do we balance our concern for human rights against the notion that states should be left alone to manage their own affairs? How can we use our diplomatic and economic influence to avoid the use of force? Should our country's policy toward intervening internationally be governed by a broad strategy, or should each case be weighed separately? Finally, should U.S. policies reflect the decisions of the UN, or should we chart our own course? This chapter will help prepare you to consider these questions.

Origins of the International Community

The concept of an "international community" began with the emergence of nation-states in Western Europe at the end of the Middle Ages. As England, France, Spain, and other nation-states grew in wealth and power, the unifying authority of the Roman Catholic Church weakened. Rather than thinking of themselves as part of one Christendom, European monarchs increasingly sought to promote the interests of their own nation-states.

In the new environment, national rulers were forced to consider problems of international relations. The greatest progress came as a result of war. The Thirty Years War (1618-48) was a critical turning point. Millions died from warfare and starvation as marauding armies laid waste to much of central Europe. From the horrors of battle came a new international consensus. Thereafter, European leaders avoided inflaming the religious passions that had fed the Thirty Years War.

The next large-scale war in Europe did not occur until the rise of Napoleon Bonaparte. The Napoleonic Wars of 1796-1815 illustrated the deadly power of new military technologies and, like the Thirty Years War, resulted in enormous destruction. When Napoleon was finally defeated in 1815, statesmen once again sought to shape an international system that would prevent future wars.

A new international system

From 1815 to 1914, the great powers of the age, known as the Concert of Europe, ruled the global system. As European countries extended their influence throughout the world, the Concert increasingly governed international affairs. Peace treaties were signed, the map of the Balkans was redrawn, and Africa was divided among European colonial empires. The International Peace Conferences at The Hague in 1899 and 1907 added a new dimension to the international system. Far-sighted participants spoke of one day bringing together all the countries of the world.

World War I swept away the self-confidence and optimism that Europe's statesmen had developed during the 19th century. Many observers asserted that diplomatic miscalculation had triggered the conflict and that regular international conferences with procedures for conflict resolution could have prevented World War I.

President Woodrow Wilson shared this belief. In January 1918, he unveiled his fourteen-

SECTION 1

A new era

When the Cold War died out in the late 1980s, the international system that had prevailed since World War II went with it. The threat of nuclear war between the superpowers faded, while small-scale civil wars and smoldering

point proposal to reshape international relations. Central to Wilson's plan were self-determination, open diplomacy, freedom of the seas, free trade, and arms limitation. A permanent global organization — the League of Nations — was to continue along the path of progress laid down by the prewar conferences at The Hague and oversee the new international system.

Wilson's idealism, however, ran up against British and French efforts to use the League as a means to protect their interests. At the same time, the U.S. Senate defied Wilson and rejected American participation in the League.

After the League of Nations treaty took effect in 1920, the organization's structural flaws became more apparent. The requirement that all League members agree to important decisions often blocked action. The exclusion of important nations, such as Germany and the Soviet Union, also limited the organization's scope. In addition, critics argued that the League was largely a tool of Britain and France.

Confronted with its first major challenge in 1931, the League failed to stop the Japanese invasion of Manchuria. Later in the 1930s, it proved powerless in the face of Italian and German aggression. By the time World War II

began, international statesmen had all but given up on the League of Nations.

The United Nations

In October 1943, with World War II still raging, the United States, the Soviet Union, Britain, and China agreed in principle to replace the defunct League with a new body, the United Nations. The four leading Allies, along with France, were largely responsible for the development of the UN's structure and became permanent members of the organization's Security Council — each with veto power over UN decisions. The Security Council was assigned primary responsibility for maintaining international peace and security. In June 1945, fifty-five nations signed the UN Charter in San Francisco.

By the late 1940s, the bitter divisions of the Cold War had overwhelmed the carefully laid plans of the UN's founders. Because of the veto system, U.S.-Soviet hostility often prevented the Security Council from making decisions. Wherever key U.S. and Soviet interests clashed, there was little hope of resolving conflicts through UN mechanisms. Nonetheless, the UN undertook thirteen peacekeeping operations from 1948 to 1987. ❏

Wayne Stayskal in the *Tampa Tribune*. Reprinted by permission: Tribune Media Services.

"WE MUST BE GOING TO WAR... WE'RE NOT ARMED HEAVILY ENOUGH FOR A PEACE-KEEPING MISSION!"

territorial disputes — most often within states rather than between states — captured international attention. Several ethnic conflicts on the fringes of the former Soviet bloc that had been smothered by the heavy hand of the communist system reignited. Other areas, especially where borders had been drawn by European colonial powers, emerged as powder kegs of conflict.

At the same time, the end of the Cold War brought new possibilities for international compromise and cooperation. For the first time since World War II, the UN was not paralyzed by division. After the late 1980s, the United States and the Soviet Union (later Russia) worked together through the UN to resolve conflicts in areas where they had once shipped weapons to opposing forces. Afghanistan, Central America, and other hot spots were no longer seen as regional contests between the United States and the Soviet Union. In El Salvador, for example, outside support for both the pro-American government and the pro-communist rebels dried up, and the two sides signed a UN-sponsored peace agreement in 1991.

Greater demand for UN support

Increasingly, the UN has been given the responsibility for maintaining peace. In 1987, the UN was directing five peacekeeping operations with 10,000 soldiers and an annual budget of $233 million. By 1994, the UN's peacekeeping role had expanded to include seventeen operations involving 73,000 soldiers at a cost of $3.6 billion a year. The two biggest operations — in the former Yugoslavia and Somalia — were each supported by more than 25,000 troops.

The UN itself does not have an army. Rather, the organization must rely on member countries to provide troops and financial support. No country is more important to UN peacekeeping efforts than the United States. The United States is capable of contributing highly trained soldiers with the latest weaponry to UN operations. Furthermore, Americans pay 30 percent of the bill for UN peacekeeping.

Advocates of the UN urge leaders worldwide to fulfill the original goals of the UN Charter to protect international peace. The changing nature of conflict, however, has led others to question the relevance of a document drawn up in the mid-1940s.

The founders of the UN saw their primary task as resolving conflicts between states. They had witnessed the failure of the League of Nations to stop the aggression of Germany and Japan against their neighbors. Skeptics note that conflicts on the UN agenda in the 1990s rarely fit the old model.

Rethinking UN operations

UN peacekeeping efforts in the post-Cold War era are expected to accomplish increasingly ambitious tasks. In Cambodia, for example, the United Nations has been called upon to oversee elections, sponsor peace talks among warring factions, resettle refugees, and rebuild state institutions such as the police force and army. In short, the United Nations is often given responsibility for picking up the pieces of a country that has fallen apart.

The job of UN peacekeepers is frequently made more difficult by the presence of free-wheeling militias that ignore government authority. When UN peacekeepers took up positions in 1948 in the Middle East and Kashmir, they could count on the discipline and order of the armies involved. In contrast, UN forces in Somalia in 1993-94 found themselves caught in the crossfire of rival groups that showed little respect for negotiated agreements. Rather than acting as a neutral party, UN troops were instructed to punish forces that threatened peace. With little advance warning, they were forced to become peacemakers rather than peacekeepers.

SECTION 2

Current case studies

The Persian Gulf War marked a definitive end to the bipolar international system of the Cold War. For the first time in UN history, the world's leading powers stood together to oppose an act of international aggression. Within hours of Iraq's invasion of Kuwait, the UN Security Council demanded an immediate withdrawal. An economic blockade soon followed. In January 1991, twenty-eight countries participated in the U.S.-led coalition that defeated Iraqi dictator Saddam Hussein.

The Persian Gulf War represented a victory for the founding ideals of the UN and raised hopes that the original goals of the UN Charter would serve as the basis for international relations in the post-Cold War world. The lessons of the war, however, have proven limited. Less than two years after orchestrating the international community's response to Saddam Hussein, President George Bush sent 25,000 American troops to Somalia at the urging of the UN to safeguard international relief efforts. Instead of establishing a successful model for outside intervention, the Somalia operation turned many Americans against international involvement. The American public was particularly outraged by a clash in October 1993 between U.S. forces and a Somali militia that left eighteen Americans and 300 Somalis dead. By the time the last American troops withdrew from the East African country in March 1994, Somalia was slipping toward chaos. The remaining members of the UN force were evacuated from the country in March 1995.

The contrasting experiences of the United States in the Persian Gulf and Somalia have shaped the debate about our country's role in international intervention in the post-Cold War era. In fighting against Iraq, well-defined military goals and effective international coordination helped American leaders rally public support behind U.S. involvement. The Somalia mission, however, lacked the clear sense of purpose of a conventional war, leaving many Americans frustrated and angry.

Foreign policy analysts predict that the international challenges the United States will confront in the future will more often resemble Somalia than Iraq. That means that American troops will increasingly be called upon to act more like policemen than soldiers, and that American leaders will face a growing list of requests from the international community for U.S. foreign aid and mediation services. As a nation, we can expect more difficult choices ahead about when and where to commit U.S. resources. In the following pages, you will examine four current conflicts that bring into sharper focus the questions surrounding the U.S. role in international intervention.

Bosnia

The conflict in Bosnia (or Bosnia-Herzegovina) has presented the Western alliance with its most crucial test since the Berlin Wall came down. Beginning in December 1995, the first North Atlantic Treaty Organization (NATO) army in history has taken responsibility for maintaining a fragile peace in Bosnia. The first year of the operation was credited with stopping the fighting that had raged for three and one-half years, but the larger goals of the United States and its allies remained in doubt. As Americans looked toward the future, the divisions of the war were as sharp as ever, and prospects for a united, peaceful Bosnia seemed distant.

U.S. involvement in Bosnia has drawn Americans closer to a region with a long history of fiery nationalism and war. Bosnia is located in the middle of the Balkan peninsula, and was once one of Europe's most ethnically mixed areas. International attention turned to Bosnia shortly after the Soviet Union fell apart. Like the republics of the former Soviet Union, Bosnia had been part of a multi-ethnic communist country. As in the Soviet Union, communism had masked many of Yugoslavia's ethnic problems. In both countries, the late 1980s saw old wounds reopen.

Yugoslavia, which means the land of the South Slavs, was formed by the international statesmen who redrew the map of Europe after World War I. In fact, the peoples of Yugoslavia had never been united by a single national identity. During the 1920s and 1930s, little progress was made in promoting unity among the Yugoslavs. Nazi occupation of Yugoslavia in World War II opened a period of terrible bloodshed. More than 1 million people died in the country during the war, many of them at the hands of their fellow Yugoslavs. By 1945, the defeat of the Nazis and a cruel civil war had brought communist leader Marshal Tito to power.

Tito's iron-fisted rule and popularity as a wartime hero held Yugoslavia together during the Cold War. Under Tito, a complex federal system distributed political power among Yugoslavia's ethnic groups. After Tito's death in 1980, however, the country's power-sharing arrangement fell apart and a period of political and economic crisis began. In the republic of Serbia, Slobodan Milosevic gained power in 1987 and pledged to promote Serbian rights. Milosevic's moves to assert Serbia's dominance in turn fed nationalism in Yugoslavia's other republics. In 1991 and 1992, the republics of Slovenia, Croatia, Bosnia, and Macedonia declared independence. Fighting

A UN soldier on patrol in Bosnia.

erupted in Slovenia and Croatia in 1991 before spilling over into Bosnia in early 1992. (Only two republics — Serbia and Montenegro — remained part of Yugoslavia.)

Bosnia had been Yugoslavia's most ethnically mixed republic — a "little Yugoslavia" where Bosnian Muslim, Serb, and Croat communities lived side by side in mountain villages. In Bosnia's capital of Sarajevo, the site of the 1984 Winter Olympics, the three groups shared one of Europe's most ethnically diverse cities.

While Bosnia's Muslims and Croats supported the creation of an independent Bosnian state, local Serbs feared they would be subject to persecution. Once fighting broke out, the toll of the Bosnian war quickly surpassed that of the other conflicts in former Yugoslavia. Although all sides were guilty of atrocities, Bosnian Serb forces were responsible for most of the brutality against civilians. The Serbs sought to eliminate Muslims and Croats from areas under their control. The process of "ethnic cleansing" was carried out through torture, gang rape, concentration camps, and massacre. By 1993, Bosnian Serb forces controlled 70 percent of Bosnia's territory.

Early in 1992, the UN established a small peacekeeping force for Sarajevo, prohibited Serbian aircraft from flying over Bosnia, and imposed economic sanctions on Milosevic's government. The UN also blocked arms shipments to all parties involved in the fighting. (The arms embargo gave the Bosnian Serbs, who received weapons from the Yugoslav army under Milosevic, a clear advantage over the poorly armed Bosnian Muslims.)

Over the next three years, international

involvement in Bosnia steadily deepened. The UN established seven "safe areas" and by the end of 1993 had increased the number of peacekeeping troops to 13,000. But while the UN issued strongly worded resolutions, there was no military commitment to back them up. UN forces on the ground were caught in a state of limbo. Their mission called on them to protect the delivery of humanitarian relief, and yet they were not equipped to counter Bosnian Serb aggression.

The Bosnian conflict entered a new stage in 1994. In February, U.S. pilots led air strikes against Bosnian Serb positions. The raids, carried out by NATO, marked the first time the international community had carried through on a threat to use force in Bosnia. Fearing more attacks, Bosnian Serb forces agreed to stop shelling Sarajevo and to move their heavy guns beyond the range of the city.

On the diplomatic front, Bosnian Croats and Muslims signed an agreement to end their ten months of fighting and form a federation in Bosnia loosely tied to Croatia. At the same time, the United States, Britain, France, Germany, and Russia worked together to press for a negotiated settlement. They unveiled a new peace plan in July 1994. Under the proposal, the Muslim-led Bosnian government would control 51 percent of Bosnia's territory, while the Bosnian Serbs would govern the remaining 49 percent.

Prospects for peace, however, appeared remote until a dramatic turn of events in 1995. Ironically, the Bosnian Serbs were responsible for setting off the chain of developments that sent them into retreat. In the spring of 1995, the Bosnian Serbs took UN peacekeepers as hostages to thwart NATO bombing raids against their positions. Many of the hostages were chained to likely bombing targets. In July, the Bosnian Serbs overran two safe areas in eastern Bosnia. Evidence soon surfaced indicating that they had executed thousands of Muslim men from the safe area Srebrenica.

The tactics of the Bosnian Serbs outraged the international community. When Croatia launched an offensive to drive Croatian Serbs out of their strongholds along the Croatian-Bosnian border, the NATO nations raised few objections.

The Croats, along with the Bosnian Muslims, quickly followed up the advance by attacking the Bosnian Serbs in western Bosnia. Meanwhile, the Bosnian Serbs again stirred the anger of the international community by killing thirty-seven civilians in an artillery barrage against Sarajevo. U.S. pilots spearheaded NATO's heaviest bombing campaign of the war, pounding the communications and supply centers of the Bosnian Serb army.

As the United States stepped up its diplomacy, a new map of Bosnia took shape. The Serb-held portion of the country shrank to 49 percent, while the Muslims extended their control to 29 percent of the territory and the Croats to 22 percent. A new military balance of power emerged as well. Both the Muslim and Serb forces were too exhausted to continue fighting, while the Croats were satisfied with the outcome.

Moreover, the ethnic cleansing that the international community had tried to prevent was mostly complete. By the fall of 1995, Bosnia consisted of three largely ethnically pure regions, each with its own army. In all, more than 200,000 people had died in the struggle for Bosnia and nearly 3 million had lost their homes. In December 1995, a formal peace agreement was signed in Dayton, Ohio.

Since the signing of the Dayton accord, the lines dividing Bosnia's Serbs, Muslims, and Croats have hardened. In elections held in September 1996, voters from the three main ethnic groups overwhelmingly supported candidates with strongly nationalistic views. International peacekeepers have been unable to enforce key aspects of the agreement, such as guarantees for freedom of movement within Bosnia and the return of refugees. Instead, thousands of additional Bosnians from all communities have been driven across the Dayton accord's dividing lines. Although seventy-five people have been indicted by the International War Crimes Tribunal, only a handful have been arrested.

The Bosnian Muslims alone support creating a united Bosnia. In contrast, the Bosnian Serbs hope to join their lands to Yugoslavia. They have linked their economy to Yugoslavia, conducting transactions with Yugoslav currency and routing international telephone calls through Belgrade. Likewise, Bosnian Croats have taken part in electing representatives to Croatia's parliament.

Despite the setbacks, the United States has pushed forward with the Dayton accord. U.S. officials hope that the grip of nationalism will eventually weaken and that the institutions of a new, multi-ethnic Bosnian state will take root. They draw encouragement from the fact that the United States did not suffer a combat death during the first eighteen months of the Bosnian mission. To back America's commitment, President Clinton dropped his pledge to withdraw U.S. peacekeeping forces from Bosnia by December 1996. Instead, Clinton offered 8,500 troops for a follow-on NATO peacekeeping force of 30,000 soldiers.

The Clinton administration hopes that the peacekeepers will provide security for a broader strategy to revive Bosnia's economy, strengthen its military, and establish an effective central government. To that end, the United States has led international efforts to raise billions of dollars of foreign aid for Bosnia. In November 1996, the United States began a program to rearm and retrain the mostly Muslim Bosnian army. Muslim nations have joined the United States in supplying the Bosnians with heavy weaponry and funding.

By the time the UN peacekeeping mission is scheduled to conclude in July 1998, U.S. officials intend to give Bosnian Muslims the ability to defend themselves. America's European allies worry that U.S. aid may transform the Bosnian Muslims from victims to aggressors. Whatever the results, even the best intentions may not be enough to prevent another round of fighting. A majority of Bosnians from all ethnic backgrounds predict that their fragile country's map will yet again be redrawn by blood.

The Kurds in northern Iraq

Since the Persian Gulf War ended in 1991, 3.7 million Kurds have depended largely on the international community to protect them from the Iraqi army and to provide them with relief supplies. The UN operation in northern Iraq set an important precedent by intervening in a sovereign state for humanitarian purposes, thus paving the way for similar actions in Somalia and the former Yugoslavia.

For the moment, northern Iraq's Kurds are governing themselves in an area of 15,000 square miles (less than half the size of South Carolina). To the south of the Kurdish zone, however, Iraqi troops remain positioned for attack. The Kurds have made little progress in establishing effective self-government. Instead, they have largely been reduced to pawns in the regional power struggle involving the United States, Iraq's Saddam Hussein, and Iraq's neighbors.

The Kurds, an ancient people of the Middle East, live by the adage:

"The mountains are our only friends." More than 20 million Kurds are scattered over five countries in the Middle East. The largest group, about 12 million, lives in Turkey, while another 5 million Kurds are based in Iran and 4.5 million in Iraq. The Kurds constitute the largest ethnic group in the Middle East without a state of their own.

The Kurds have been among the chief losers in the political changes that have swept over the Middle East in the 20th century. The Kurds failed to achieve statehood at the end of World War I when the Allied powers redrew the map of the defeated Ottoman Turkish empire. Although Kurdish nationalists lobbied President Wilson and other Western leaders, their interests were ignored in the final peace settlement.

During the Cold War, the Kurds served largely as a tool of U.S. and Soviet policy in the Middle East. In the early 1970s, Kurdish guerrillas received American assistance to press their campaign for autonomy against the pro-Soviet regime in Iraq. In 1974, however, U.S. aid was suddenly stopped at the request of the shah of Iran, an American ally. The Kurdish guerrilla movement was then subject to a war of extermination orchestrated by Saddam Hussein. An estimated 4,200 Kurdish villages were destroyed by the Iraqi army. At least 180,000 Kurds were forced out of their homeland, either dying at the hands of Iraqi soldiers or crowded into camps in southern Iraq. The most well-known incident of Saddam's brutality took place in 1988, when Iraq's air force dropped poison gas on the town of Halabja. At least 5,000 people were killed in the attack.

The Persian Gulf War opened a new chapter in Kurdish history. With the quick defeat of Iraq's army by the U.S.-led coalition in early 1991, the Kurds of northern Iraq saw an opportunity to overthrow Saddam Hussein. Along with Shi'ite Muslims in southern Iraq and other opposition forces, Kurdish guerrillas renewed their rebellion against the Iraqi army. International support for the rebellion, however, evaporated after Saudi Arabia, Turkey, and other Middle Eastern states voiced concern that the disintegration of Iraq would destabilize the region.

With the shift in international attitudes, Saddam Hussein concentrated the remainder of his army on smashing the Kurdish resistance. The Iraqi advance pushed nearly 2 million panicked Kurds across the border into Turkey and Iran. Hundreds died in snowy mountain passes and makeshift refugee camps. In response to the crisis, 20,000 troops from the U.S.-led coalition carved out a security zone for the Kurds near the Turkish border. They also warned that Iraqi warplanes flying north of the 36th parallel

Kurdish refugees from northern Iraq receive UN food aid.

would be shot down. In a matter of days, a UN-authorized safe haven had been created mostly by U.S. forces.

Since 1991, the Kurds of northern Iraq have been caught in the middle of a test of wills between the United States and Iraq. Saddam Hussein's government has worked to regain control over northern Iraq by sowing division among the Kurds. The strategy has proved successful. Thousands of Kurds have died in fighting among themselves.

In August 1996, the Kurdistan Democratic Party (KDP) invited more than 30,000 Iraqi troops to join in its struggle against a rival faction, the Patriotic Union of Kurdistan. Iraq's incursion prompted the United States to launch two missile attacks against Iraqi air-defense installations in southern Iraq. Iraqi troops soon retreated from northern Iraq, but by then the future of the safe haven seemed more doubtful than ever. Fighting among the Kurds continued for over a month before the United States brokered a cease-fire.

The economy of northern Iraq is just as desperate as the political situation. Although Saddam Hussein lifted Iraq's economic blockade against areas controlled by the KDP, about one-third of the population in northern Iraq remains dependent on international humanitarian assistance. Trade is mostly limited to items that can be trucked in across the borders of Turkey and Iran. At the same time, the Turkish government has applied heavy-handed measures of its own to defeat Kurdish rebels in eastern Turkey. In the spring of 1997, more than 10,000 Turkish troops drove into northern Iraq to flush out the rebels.

U.S. officials weigh the American position in northern Iraq largely in terms of their efforts to contain Saddam Hussein. So far, Washington has been willing to counter each of Saddam's moves. Nonetheless, the costs are mounting. U.S. pilots flying out of a NATO air base in Turkey are largely responsible for enforcing the no-fly zone in northern Iraq. In addition, the United States has been supplying the Kurds about $130 million worth of humanitarian aid annually.

Rwanda and Burundi

In the spring of 1994, a world long accustomed to conflict was shocked by the violence that engulfed the central African country of Rwanda. In the span of a few weeks, as many as 500,000 members of the Tutsi minority were slaughtered by their fellow Rwandans. Evidence quickly mounted that Hutu extremists within the government were bent on genocide. Nonetheless, the international community waited for months before intervening in Rwanda.

Tragically, the events of the spring of 1994 were only one chapter in one of the world's bloodiest and most explosive conflicts. Since gaining independence in 1962, Rwanda and the neighboring state of Burundi have been torn by strife between the Tutsis and the Hutus. For the moment, the Tutsis dominate both countries. The ethnic balance, however, suggests that there is further trouble ahead. In both Rwanda and Burundi, the Hutus make up at least 85 percent of the population, while the Tutsis are less than 15 percent.

The hostility between Hutus and Tutsis, however intense, reaches back only a few decades. The two groups share the same culture, language, and religion. Physically, they are virtually indistinguishable from one another. The main differences between them are economic. Although a minority, the Tutsis have long held most of the land. For centuries, they were primarily cattle herders while the Hutus were farmers. Under German and then Belgian colonial rule, the economic differences were deepened. The Belgians openly favored the Tutsis, reserving educational privileges and government jobs solely for them.

In the late 1950s, the Belgians hastily organized elections in Rwanda and Burundi as their colonial empire began to crumble. Hutu parties gained control of the Rwandan government in 1959, triggering armed opposition by the Tutsis. In three years of civil war, 50,000 Rwandans were killed and another 100,000 (almost all Tutsi) fled the country. In Burundi, the Tutsis took advantage of their control of the army to override election results and seize political power. During the next three decades, Burundi's Tutsi-led government crushed repeated Hutu uprisings. In 1972, as many as 100,000 Hutus were killed.

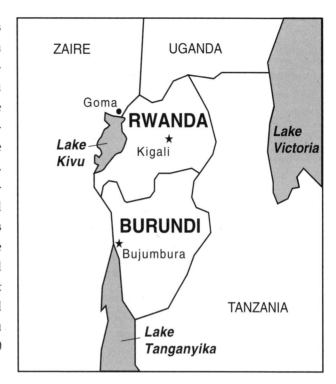

Their ethnic conflict notwithstanding, the vast majority of Hutus and Tutsis alike struggled for survival as small farmers after the end of colonial rule. By 1994, Rwanda, with a population of 8.4 million people, and Burundi, with 6.2 million people, were among the world's most densely populated and poorest nations. (Each country is about the size of Maryland.) Poverty and the scarcity of land played into the hands of politicians seeking to ignite ethnic tensions to further their power. In 1990, the region's problems were further complicated by the invasion of the Rwandan Patriotic Front. A small-scale civil war generated a fresh wave of refugees. Most of the soldiers in the rebel army were Tutsi refugees who had been living in neighboring Uganda since the early 1960s.

In August 1993, a peace agreement between the rebels and the government was signed and a small UN force was put in place to oversee the accord. Events in Burundi, however, soon reignited tensions. In October 1993, Tutsi army officers killed Burundi's first Hutu president, Melchior Ndadaye, in an attempt to overthrow the new government. Burundi was plunged into violence. As many as 100,000 people, most of them Hutus, were killed.

Hutu extremists in Rwanda used the Burundi crisis as an opportunity to fan hostility against Tutsis. In April 1994, Rwandan President Juvenal

J. Isaac. Courtesy of the United Nations.

Rwandan children separated from their parents at a refugee camp in former Zaire.

Habyarimana was killed in a suspicious plane crash, along with the president of Burundi. Within hours of the crash, the Rwandan army and specially formed Hutu militias began carrying out a well-organized series of massacres.

As the bloodbath continued, the Tutsi-led Rwandan Patriotic Front advanced against government forces. By July 1994, it had seized the capital and forced the army to flee in panic. Fearful of reprisals, hundreds of thousands of Hutus abandoned their homes.

World leaders condemned the violence in Rwanda, but balked at intervening to stop the genocide. (U.S. officials backed away from defining the killings as "genocide.") International forces, including 2,000 American troops, arrived after the massacres had ended to protect international relief operations for the nearly 2 million Hutu refugees. The last UN peacekeepers left Rwanda in early 1996.

The outpouring of refugees beyond Rwanda's borders created a new set of problems. In eastern Zaire (renamed Congo in 1997), where 1.2 million Hutus had fled, the refugee camps fell under the control of the Hutu extremists behind Rwanda's genocide. They organized a guerrilla army that staged raids against the new Tutsi-led government in Rwanda. Hutu leaders also blocked their fellow refugees from returning home.

The refugee crisis reached the boiling point in the fall of 1996. Hutu guerrillas, joining forces with the Zairian army, increasingly turned their guns on Tutsis who had been living in Zaire for centuries. When the Zairian Tutsis struck back, with the support of the Rwandan army, they overran key refugee camps at Goma. Their military success exposed the weakness of the Zairian army and generated momentum for a larger Zairian uprising against the regime of Mobutu Sese Seko. In a little over seven months, a rebel movement led by Laurent Kabila drove across Zaire and forced Mobutu into exile.

While Rwandan President Paul Kagame applauded Kabila's victory, the problems facing his country have continued. Kabila's uprising prompted at least 1 million Hutu refugees to abandon their camps in eastern Zaire and return to Rwanda. Officially, Kagame's government has welcomed them back, but Rwanda's leadership fears that many will join the Hutu militias battling the Rwandan army.

In neighboring Burundi, violence between the Tutsi-led army and Hutu militias has left even deeper wounds. After the death of President Ndadaye in October 1993, order in Burundi all but collapsed. A coalition government formed in 1994 was unable to build cooperation between Hutus and Tutsis. In July 1996, a Tutsi army officer, Pierre Buyoya, seized power and promised to stop the bloodshed. Many Hutus, however, blamed Buyoya for masterminding the assassination of Ndadaye.

An economic embargo imposed by neighboring countries against Buyoya's regime has failed to bring Burundi closer to peace. Instead, concern is mounting that the violence in Burundi may escalate. With that in mind, President Clinton has pledged U.S. funding to train and equip a quick-response peacekeeping force drawn from African nations.

Haiti

Haitian history bears the marks of political turmoil, poverty, and U.S. intervention. The latest round of U.S. military involvement in Haiti may signal a turning point. For the first time, Haiti is being run by a popularly elected democratic leader and the rule of law has generally replaced dictatorial brutality. Haitians themselves, however, are skeptical about their nation's direction. They question if their fledgling democracy will take root and grow, or if Haiti's recent accomplishments will crumble once international forces leave their island. As in the past, much of Haiti's future hinges on U.S. policy.

Haiti's 6.5 million people share the Caribbean island of Hispaniola with the Dominican Republic. The French began colonizing the island in the 16th century, bringing in African slaves to work their plantations. In 1804, Haiti gained independence from France after slaves organized a successful revolt. Haiti's rulers, however, failed to establish a stable political system on the island. In 1915, U.S. Marines landed in Haiti to establish order and ensure that the island did not fall under German influence. The Marines remained until 1934, leaving behind a country that was administered chiefly by the military.

From 1957 to 1986, Haiti was governed by Francois "Papa Doc" Duvalier and his son Jean Claude "Baby Doc" Duvalier. The Duvalier dynasty brought a measure of political stability to Haiti, but the great majority of Haitians saw little improvement in their lives. Increasingly, Haitian society was divided between a small, educated elite in the well-kept neighborhoods of Port-au-Prince, Haiti's capital, and a huge poverty-stricken class of illiterate farmers and slum dwellers. Duvalier's police force and army maintained the social structure through a combination of brutality, intimidation, and voodoo. Haiti became the poorest country in the Western Hemisphere.

The corruption of Baby Doc Duvalier ultimately triggered his downfall

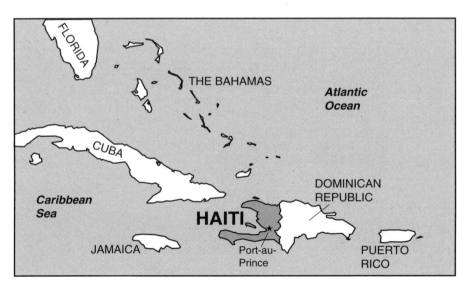

Bettmann

Haitians rally in support of Jean-Bertrand Aristide.

in 1986. After Duvalier fled to France, however, Haiti's troubles continued. A series of military leaders laid claim to power but lacked the strength to establish control over the government. Meanwhile, a grassroots movement for democracy slowly gathered momentum among Haiti's poor.

With the support of the international community, Haiti held its first fully democratic election in 1990. The results were a rejection of the old elite. Jean-Bertrand Aristide, a Roman Catholic priest closely identified with the democracy movement, won 67 percent of the vote in a field of eleven candidates. His promise to reorganize the army and police force, clamp down on corruption, and reform the economy stirred hope among Haiti's poor. Aristide's platform, however, terrified the country's ruling class. In September 1991, the old elite engineered a military coup that forced Aristide to flee the country.

The international community united against the army officers who deposed Aristide. The Organization of American States, to which thirty-five countries in the Western Hemisphere belong, imposed an economic embargo on Haiti. From 1990 to 1994, Haiti's economy shrank by nearly one-third.

As conditions in Haiti worsened, thousands of Haitians set out across the Caribbean, hoping to reach U.S. territory. Although some were granted refugee status, the majority were returned to Haiti or were turned back at sea by the U.S. Coast Guard. Human rights groups estimate that in 1991-93 the Haitian government killed as many as 3,000 of its citizens and forced 40,000 to flee the country.

In 1994, the UN extended its trade embargo to cover virtually all goods other than food and medicine. The defiance of the coup leaders and the continued exodus of Haitian "boat people" toward the United States led President Clinton to favor military action. He pressed for the passage of a resolution in the UN Security Council that backed the use of force to restore President Aristide to office. By September 1994, Clinton was prepared to launch an invasion force of 20,000 soldiers against Haiti's rulers.

A last-minute agreement allowed U.S. troops to enter Haiti without opposition. Placing U.S. forces on the island, however, was only the first step in re-establishing a democratic government. The Americans soon confronted the task of restoring order to Haitian society. Thousands of weapons were collected, and programs were set up to train a new police force and army.

The first stage of the international operation left U.S. officials cautiously optimistic. The U.S.-led invasion force quickly gave way to a 6,000-man UN unit dominated by 2,500 American troops. Violence was sharply reduced throughout the island. The outflow of boat people slowed to a trickle. Despite fearful warnings, not a single American soldier was killed in combat. In fact, the great majority of Haitians clearly supported the international presence. In turn, Aristide won praise for his moderation. He rejected calls to punish Haiti's elite and instead reached out to include representatives of the country's business community in his government. In February 1996, the UN force was pared down to 1,550 peacekeepers and is likely to end its mission in late 1997.

Calm in Haiti, however, rests on weak underpinnings. The economy has shown few signs of improvement. Outside investment has been meager and nearly three-quarters of the island nation's workers are unemployed. Hunger continues to stalk the countryside. Seventy percent of the government's budget consists of foreign aid. Plans to privatize state-run industries have sparked protest. Moreover, few of the officials who terrorized Haiti's population before Aristide's return have been brought to justice.

Politically, Haiti's democracy appears shaky as well. Killings of police officers and assassination threats against government officials continue to mar Haiti's development. Rivalry between Aristide and Rene Preval, who was elected to the presidency in 1996, has hobbled the effectiveness of the government.

To prevent Haiti from again slipping into chaos, the United States has increasingly chosen to act on its own. Since 1996, the United States has maintained a separate force of 500 troops on the island. On several occasions, the Clinton administration has used America's military presence to protect Preval's administration. Both U.S. and Haitian officials, however, recognize that short-term fixes will not remedy Haiti's ills. On the contrary, lasting change may require many years of reform.

SECTION 3

Views on U.S. options

Now that you have read about some of the issues related to U.S. policy on conflict resolution and considered four case studies, it is time to take a closer look at what our country's position should be. In this section, you will explore four views on U.S. policy toward international intervention. As you will see, each of the views is based on a distinct set of values and beliefs, and is shaped by a well-defined perspective on the threats and opportunities facing the United States.

The views presented address three fundamental questions that frame the discussion on U.S. policy:

•**When should the United States intervene in international conflicts?** Should the United States take action only when U.S. interests are directly affected? Or should the United States become involved to stop genocide, ethnic cleansing, and other egregious violations of human rights?

•**What should be our country's relationship with the international community in the area of conflict resolution?** Should the United States contribute troops to a UN peacekeeping force and intervene abroad only in conjunction with the UN? Or should the United States set an independent course and refuse to place American troops under UN command?

•**What should be the main goal of U.S. policy regarding international conflicts?** Should U.S. involvement in international conflicts be limited to stopping the fighting and containing threats to U.S. interests? Or should the United States seek to address the root causes of conflict and to achieve a just settlement?

Each of the four views that follows responds differently to these questions. You should think of the views as a tool designed to help you examine the contrasting strategies from which Americans must define our country's role in the world and craft future policy.

View 1 — Cooperate to strengthen the UN

The international community is poised as never before to work together to address global problems. The great powers now share a common interest in promoting peace and tackling the issues that affect the entire planet. At this historic juncture, the United States should focus its energies on strengthening the United Nations — the only institution capable of addressing the challenges of the 21st century. We should join ranks with other countries under the UN umbrella to devise a comprehensive strategy to respond promptly to the world's many conflicts. The international community must let the world's aggressors know that they will be punished.

Considering trade-offs

• Will turning over decision-making power to the UN undercut the ability of the United States to respond swiftly and decisively to international crises, especially when Russia, China, or other UN Security Council members are involved?

• Will placing American soldiers under UN command result in our country's troops dying in conflicts that are of no interest to the United States?

• Will giving the UN the green light to expand its peacekeeping operations require American taxpayers to pay billions of additional dollars to support efforts that may not address U.S. interests?

View 2 — Protect our interests

With the end of the Cold War, the United States must now pick its way through a complex tangle of shifting alliances and conflicting interests. In the matter of intervening abroad, that means that the United States must carefully choose how and where to get involved. The United States needs to maintain important trading partnerships, control the spread of nuclear weapons, and prevent a flood of refugees from overwhelming us and our allies. Our judgment must not be clouded by the latest television newscasts. Ultimately, we must do what is required to protect U.S. interests.

Considering trade-offs

• Will intervening in the affairs of other countries on our own entangle the United States in long-term, no-win disputes?

• Will strictly pursuing our own interests in international intervention harm our relations with other countries in the UN and weaken the international system?

• Will intervening in a conflict to defend narrow U.S. interests provoke Russia, China, and other great powers to likewise intervene to protect their own national interests?

View 3 — Keep our distance

Since the late 1940s, the United States has stuck its nose into problems around the world. The obsession with foreign affairs has come at the expense of dealing with our problems here at home. For the rest of the world, our pattern of intervention has not brought peace and prosperity. Today, we must strike a new balance between foreign policy and domestic issues. The United States should not take part in UN efforts to intervene in conflict areas. The extent of our involvement in conflict resolution should be limited to the Western Hemisphere. We must recognize that the peace and stability of the world is best served by respecting the principles of state sovereignty and territorial integrity.

Considering trade-offs

• Will cutting our ties to UN peacekeeping efforts undermine the ability of the international community to deal with other global problems, such as environmental pollution and health epidemics?

• Will ignoring conflicts outside of the Western Hemisphere come back to haunt us in the form of broken trade relations, refugee crises, threats to our raw material supplies, and nuclear proliferation?

• Will our failure to play an active role in the international arena embolden the enemies of democratic values and human rights?

View 4 — Stand up for principle

Since our country was founded, the world has turned to the United States for inspiration and leadership. We have led the way in developing a society based on democracy and liberty. Today, the United States has a greater role than ever to play in the world. As the only remaining superpower, we are in a position to advance the American values of democracy and human rights throughout the globe. The United States should let the world know that we will take the lead in intervening abroad to support democratic movements and punish brutal dictators. We must exercise leadership, not get caught up in the endless debates of the UN.

Considering trade-offs

• Will taking the lead in resolving the world's conflicts force us to maintain a huge military and require American troops to fight alone in remote areas that do not affect our national interests?

• Will trying to uphold American values in the international arena bring us into conflict with powerful nations, such as China, damage our relations with key trading partners in the Persian Gulf and elsewhere, and destroy the fragile UN consensus on conflict resolution that has recently emerged?

• Will taking a threatening stance against non-democratic governments harm our ability to communicate with the very countries most likely to be involved in conflicts?

Your turn

These views are by no means the only U.S. options. Rather, they are intended to lay out some of the most important values and assumptions underlying the debate on U.S. policy concerning conflicts abroad and to spur discussion on the direction our country should take regarding this pressing issue. When you meet next time, you will have an opportunity to discuss the U.S. role in international intervention with others. The following statements are designed to help you clarify your thoughts on what is most important to you concerning this issue. Take a few moments to respond. This is a tool for you to get started. It will not be collected.

Rate each of the statements according to your beliefs:

1 = Strongly Support	3 = Oppose	5 = Undecided
2 = Support	4 = Strongly Oppose	

___ The interests of the United States can be maintained only if we resolutely exercise our power and influence in international affairs.

___ The international community has an obligation to intervene in countries that do not respect accepted standards of human rights.

___ Using our military power independently of the international community creates more enemies than friends.

___ Problems in the international arena are far less important for Americans than the challenges we face at home, such as poverty, crime, and budget deficits.

___ The United States should recognize that problems in the developing world, such as poverty and environmental degradation, must be addressed as problems that affect everyone on the planet.

___ The world would be a better place if more countries were to adopt our country's democratic values.

___ International stability and order should be protected because they are vital to the interests of the United States.

___ The United States should be willing to give up some of its own sovereignty to promote international cooperation.

___ Involving ourselves in the affairs of other countries is wasteful and dangerous.

Suggested reading

Damrosch, Lori Fisler, ed. *Enforcing Restraint: Collective Intervention in Internal Conflicts* (New York: Council on Foreign Relations Press, 1993).

Ignatieff, Michael. *Blood and Belonging: Journeys into the New Nationalism* (New York: Farrar, Straus, and Giroux, 1994).

Kaplan, Robert D. *The Ends of the Earth: From Togo to Turkmenistan, from Iran to Cambodia, a Journey to the Frontiers of Anarchy* (New York: Vintage Books, 1997).

Little, Alan and Silber, Laura. *Yugoslavia: Death of a Nation* (New York: Penguin Books, 1996).

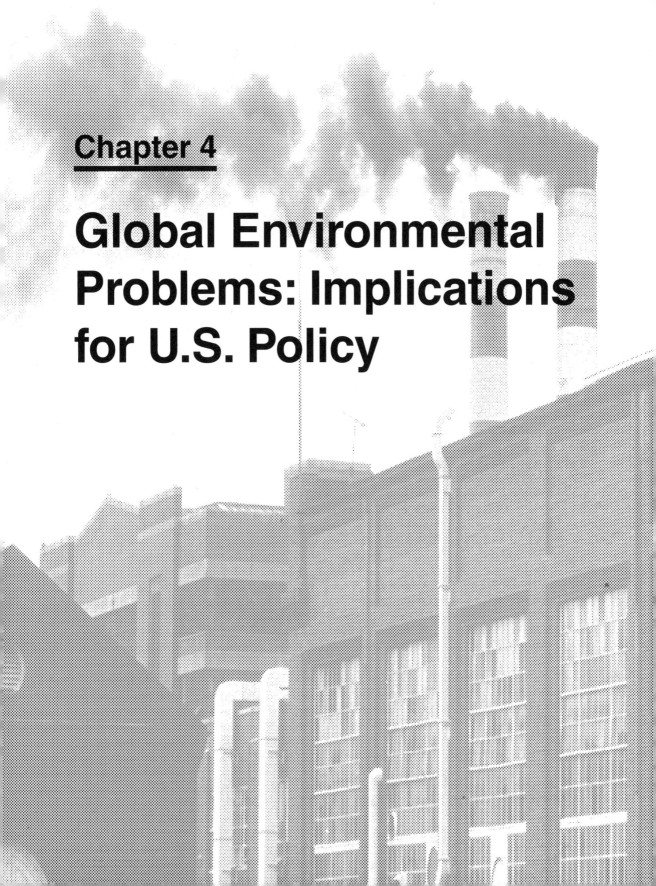

Chapter 4

Global Environmental Problems: Implications for U.S. Policy

In the fall of 1995, a United Nations scientific panel announced that years of research and mounting evidence had led the group to an inescapable conclusion: human activity was altering the earth's climate. The Intergovernmental Panel on Climate Change, which includes 2,500 scientists from around the world, reported that the increase of average global surface temperatures by about 1 degree Fahrenheit in the last century was most likely attributable to industrialization, and that still warmer weather was forecast for the 21st century.

The data brought to light by the panel indeed warrants worldwide

Global Environmental Problems

To understand why ecological concerns have become part of the international as well as the domestic agenda, we must examine how environmental threats affect life on the planet. The following section summarizes the causes and possible consequences of five critical environmental problems: global warming, ozone depletion, acid rain, deforestation and desertification, and the decline of biodiversity.

Global warming

Much of the current anxiety regarding environmental problems has revolved around global warming. Scientists have linked the process to the buildup of carbon dioxide, methane, nitrogen oxides, chlorofluorocarbons (CFCs), and other trace gases. These gases are often referred to as "greenhouse" gases because of the way they trap heat in the atmosphere.

Carbon dioxide has received the most attention from scientists. Carbon dioxide not only sustains plant life, but also absorbs much of the earth's infrared (long-wave) energy that would otherwise be radiated back into space. By absorbing heat, carbon dioxide keeps the earth warm enough to support life. Humanity, however, has added carbon dioxide to the atmosphere by burning fossil fuels such as oil, coal, and natural gas. Since the start of the Industrial Revolution, the amount of carbon dioxide in the atmosphere has increased by 25 percent.

The UN's Intergovernmental Panel on Climate Change predicts that average global temperatures will rise between 1.8 degrees and 6.3 degrees Fahrenheit by 2100 unless greenhouse gas emissions are curbed. If the projections prove correct, people in the next century would have to cope with more heat waves, floods, droughts, and fires. Global warming would make desert climates more extreme and wipe out vast swaths of forest. Moreover, the UN panel forecasts that global warming over the next century would raise the level of the world's seas by about 20 inches as the polar icecaps melt. Nearly 20 percent of the world's population, as well as many of the planet's most fragile ecosystems, could be vulnerable to coastal flooding.

Scientists acknowledge that they have much to learn about the factors affecting the global climate, and that the computer models they use to predict future global temperatures need refinement. At the same time, science offers hope

attention, but perhaps just as important is the forum for the scientific findings. Since 1992, when 178 governments took part in the United Nations (UN) Conference on Environment and Development, global warming has been in the international spotlight. At a string of UN gatherings, analyses of carbon dioxide emissions and fossil fuel consumption have dominated discussion. By the end of 1997, world leaders are due to draw up the most specific proposals yet to prevent the planet from overheating. Future meetings and additional studies are already scheduled.

Since the earliest days of international diplomacy, states have generally come together to discuss matters of war and trade. Degradation of the

that humanity may be able to adapt to a changing climate with new seed varieties, higher sea walls, and other measures.

Ozone depletion

Since the 1970s, scientists have known that certain chemicals damage the ozone layer — the atmospheric shield ten to twenty-five miles above the earth that prevents much of the sun's damaging ultraviolet (UV) radiation from reaching the surface of the planet. In 1985, scientists discovered a hole in the ozone layer over Antarctica the size of the continental United States. By 1995, the area covered by the hole had more than doubled. Equally alarming, scientists have found a smaller hole in the ozone layer over the North Pole, leaving people in Canada and the northernmost areas of United States and Eurasia vulnerable to increased ultraviolet radiation.

Chemicals containing chlorine and bromine have been linked to the destruction of the ozone layer. When these chemicals are released into the atmosphere, they slowly rise into the stratosphere and eat away at the ozone layer for about 100 years. Of the chlorine-producing

chemicals, CFCs have the greatest impact. They are used in refrigeration, air conditioners, aerosols, upholstery, foam insulation, and packing materials. (They also contribute to global warming.) When CFCs were invented in 1928, they were hailed as a safe alternative to ammonia and other dangerous coolants used in refrigerators. No one imagined that the same chemicals posed an environmental threat.

Developed countries agreed to stop producing CFCs at the end of 1995. Nonetheless, eliminating ozone-depleting chemicals from existing equipment could take decades.

Ozone depletion could have serious consequences for human health, plants, and sea life. Greater exposure to UV radiation would result in increased rates of skin cancer, cataracts, and immune system problems. Scientists predict that additional UV radiation would also reduce crop yields and harm phytoplankton, the first link in the aquatic food chain.

Acid rain

Acid rain results from the pollutants emitted by the combustion of fossil fuels, especially coal. The leading agents of acid rain — sulfur

environment, if considered at all, was thought of strictly in a local context. Recent years, however, have witnessed a conceptual leap. Not only have scientific terms such as greenhouse gases and the ozone layer entered the public policy lexicon, but environmental problems are increasingly seen as global in scope. Whether the issue is acid rain over the Great Lakes, the destruction of the rain forest in the Amazon Basin, or desertification in the Horn of Africa, there is a growing sense that the health of the planet's ecology belongs on the international agenda.

The meetings on environmental matters also serve to highlight a widening fissure in international relations. At each of the conferences, the political battles have pitted the wealthy developed nations of the North against the poor developing countries of the South. At the Conference on Environment and Development — dubbed the "Earth Summit" — most developed countries had hoped that the gathering would be devoted

---

oxides and nitrogen oxides — are released by smokestacks, smelting plants, and automobiles. Once in the atmosphere, these pollutants are converted to acid, then return to the earth's surface as precipitation, often hundreds of miles from their source. Scientists have determined that the harmful effects of acid rain take a heavy toll on forests. Excess acids leach nutrients from forest soils and impair the ability of trees to use the remaining nutrients.

Acid rain has emerged as a controversial problem among industrialized nations. Germans, who decry the destruction of their Black Forest, claim that more than half of their acid rain originates elsewhere. Similarly, Canadians point out that the acid rain they receive from the United States is up to four times more than the amount that the United States receives from Canada. Recently, the two neighbors agreed to stricter measures to reduce sulfur oxide emissions.

Greater concern about acid rain has led many industrialized countries to control sulfur oxide pollution by promoting the use of scrubbers in coal plants and other new technologies. In the developing world, however, increased industrialization and automobile use threatens to extend the problem of acid rain to even more areas.

Deforestation and desertification

Since ancient times, people have cleared trees for agriculture and settlements. The great civilizations of the Mediterranean world devastated the woodlands of the region. The forests of Britain occupy one-tenth of the land they did 3,000 years ago.

In areas where rainfall is scarce — amounting to one-third of the earth's land — deforestation often leads to desertification. The root structure of trees holds soil in place and provides nutrients for ground cover. Conversely, clearing away trees exposes soil to the full force of rain and wind. Poor farming practices and short-sighted irrigation methods also hasten soil erosion. Livestock further degrades the land by eating young plants and leaving behind hard-packed trails and gullies.

Every year, approximately 70,000 square miles of land are taken out of production. In the

exclusively to protecting the environment. In contrast, nations of the developing world looked upon the Earth Summit as an opportunity to address the enormous gulf in wealth that separates the North from the South.

As in other international matters, the United States occupies a pivotal position in determining the world's response to global environmental problems and balancing the trade-offs of economic growth. Should we use our influence to promote international cooperation to protect the planet's ecosystem? Or should we reject strategies that strengthen the power of the UN and other international organizations? Should we join with developing countries to bridge the gap in wealth between the North and the South? Or should we narrowly focus on limiting pollution and controlling population growth in poor nations? This chapter will help prepare you to consider these questions.

1930s, grasslands of the American Great Plains that had been plowed up during the previous decade were turned into a dust bowl by drought. Today, productive land is being lost to desert primarily in Africa, where 26 percent of the continent is undergoing some form of desertification. Tropical forests also suffer. In Brazil, which contains one-quarter of the world's tropical forests, trees have been cleared in the Amazon River basin for cattle ranching, logging, and agriculture. Since tropical forests absorb much of the atmosphere's carbon dioxide and release large amounts of carbon dioxide when burned, their loss could speed up global warming.

Decline of biodiversity

Any loss of biodiversity — the range of life on the planet — is beyond human power to replace. Some biologists predict that the earth may lose one-fifth of its existing species in the next twenty years. Concern for preserving biodiversity centers particularly on areas that are rich in wildlife, such as tropical rainforests. Although they cover only 6 percent of the earth, tropical rainforests contain over half the world's species. Every year, more than 40 million acres of tropical rainforest — an area the size of Washington state — are lost, and with them 4,000 to 6,000 tropical species.

Other species-rich habitats are also endangered. Coastal wetlands have been damaged by development, while overfishing has nearly exhausted many of the ocean's most prized fishing grounds.

Environmental organizations in developed countries have been largely responsible for laws protecting endangered species. The Alaska National Interest Lands Conservation Act of 1980 set aside an area larger than California to preserve Arctic wildlife. Protecting wildlife, however, has also sparked protest from industries, such as timber and energy, that are barred from protected areas. Many developing countries, such as Kenya and Zimbabwe, are also attempting to protect wildlife by expanding their parks and preserves. In most of Africa and other poor regions, however, governments lack the funds to combat well-organized poaching operations. ❑

Determining U.S. policy

No country has as much impact on the global environment as the United States. With less than 5 percent of the world's population, the United States consumes over 20 percent of the world's energy and produces over 20 percent of the world's output of goods and services.

The American public's concern over air and water pollution first surfaced as an important political issue in the 1960s. The passage of the National Environmental Policy Act and the creation of the Environmental Protection Agency in 1970 served as an early model for other countries. The advances have been substantial. Over the past three decades, anti-pollution measures have resulted in marked improvements in air and water quality in the United States.

The election of Ronald Reagan as president in 1980 brought a more conservative outlook on environmental issues to the White House. President Reagan, and later George Bush, sought to reduce governmental regulation of the economy and, in turn, opposed environmental measures that hampered economic growth. Meanwhile, other developed nations adopted stronger environmental legislation. By 1992, limits on air pollution in Japan and Germany were nearly four times as rigorous as those in the United States.

President Bill Clinton has elevated the profile of environmental issues. He has favored tightening the enforcement of environmental regulations and bringing the United States into line with other developed countries on international environmental policy. Clinton, however, has backed away from proposals to raise fuel-efficiency standards for vehicles.

Environmentalist critics of U.S. policy warn that the most difficult ecological choices lie ahead for Americans. They insist that the United States should take stronger action to limit the destruction of natural habitats and control greenhouse gas emissions. At the opposite pole are those who argue that existing environmental regulations undermine business and infringe unfairly on the rights of property owners.

Regulations and guidelines

The United States already spends more money on the environment — just over 2 percent of the gross national product — than any other country. Most of that spending is borne by businesses in response to government regulations. The 1990 Clean Air Act, for example, requires industry to reduce emissions of sulfur oxides, nitrogen oxides, and other pollutants. In 1997, President Clinton tightened air pollution standards despite protests from industry executives and big city mayors.

Early in his administration, Clinton dropped the idea of using tax policy as an instrument for attacking pollution. Environmental advocates in the White House had initially supported taxes on the carbon content in fossil fuels, borrowing from the example set by five European countries with carbon taxes. They noted that taxes on gasoline in this country are a fraction of those in Western Europe and Japan. While Germans, for example, pay about $1.50 in taxes for a gallon of gasoline and the French pay more than $2 a gallon, U.S. consumers pay, on average, less than forty cents per gallon in state and federal taxes. Opponents of the plan, however, fear the economic impact of a carbon tax, arguing that the burden would fall heaviest on poor and middle-income automobile owners.

Since gaining a majority in Congress in 1994, Republicans have put the rollback of environmental restrictions on their legislative agenda. They have called for a moratorium on new regulations and warned Clinton against accepting UN timetables to reduce greenhouse gas emissions.

Courtesy of the Library of Congress

Promoting environmentally friendly industries

Environmental policy also touches on the government's role in the economy. Unlike President Bush, Clinton believes that the government should invest in developing environmentally sound technologies to ensure that the United States is competitive with Japan and Western Europe in the emerging "green" market.

President Clinton's initiatives include a partnership between the government and American automakers in order to produce a family-size car that would be three times more fuel-efficient than existing vehicles. In addition, the president ordered the federal government to buy paper made from at least 30 percent recycled fiber by the end of 1998.

Environmentalists want American business executives to follow the lead of Japan, where corporations are urged to prepare for a new phase of international competition by exceeding the environmental standards of foreign countries in which they operate. They note that the Japanese government is already investing in technologies designed to be environmentally friendly. At the same time, American scientists are lobbying Washington to fund research projects that promise a greener future.

Critics of such proposals are wary of a government hand in picking winners and losers among emerging technologies, arguing that free market

Per Capita Energy Consumption

Data from *The Economist*

Energy use calculated in tons of oil

competition is a better decision-maker. They contend that the cause of environmentalism is often used to camouflage the interests of those advocating expanded government control over the economy and a broader role for international organizations.

Industry has complained the loudest about the role of environmentalism in policymaking. General Motors, Ford, and Chrysler, for example, lobbied California officials to relax a law that would have mandated that 2 percent of the cars sold in the state by 1998 be pollution-free. Although General Motors began selling electric cars in California and Arizona in late 1996, the auto companies maintain that government-imposed deadlines are often unrealistic. General Motors executives forecast that they will be able to sell from 5,000 to 20,000 electric cars annually as the market gets off the ground.

Both sides of the environmental debate appreciate that the distinction between domestic and international environmental issues has become increasingly blurred. Supporters of strong environmental measures, such as a carbon tax, typically hope that the United States will cooperate closely with other members of the international community to address environmental threats. In contrast, critics of such measures fear that, in the name of environmental protection, the United States will be hamstrung by internationally mandated regulations.

SECTION 2

Dilemmas of economic development

From the earliest stages of civilization, humanity has been forced to cope with limits imposed by the earth's environment. Pastures were stripped bare, forests exhausted, and farmland eroded. Since the Industrial Revolution, we have increasingly come to view environmental constraints from a global perspective. For the first time in history, environmental problems have compelled us to ponder the limits of human activity.

At the core of the question are the issues of population growth and consumption patterns. Our planet is home to more than 5.8 billion people, with population growing at the rate of nearly 80 million a year. Almost 95 percent of population growth is occurring in developing countries. At the same time, the roughly 1 billion people of the developed world consume well over half of the world's resources. For example, the consumption rate for Americans is twenty times higher than that of South Asians or sub-Saharan Africans.

Energy Choices

In the environmental debate, energy stands out as a major issue. Particularly important are policies on conservation, environmental regulations, and the funding of research on new technologies. Environmentalists view weaning humanity off fossil fuels, which supply the world with about 90 percent of our energy, as a crucial challenge of the 21st century. They were encouraged by America's progress toward conservation after the 1973 Arab oil embargo. Spurred by higher energy prices, the United States lowered the national speed limit and adopted fuel efficiency standards for cars. Since the fall of energy prices in the mid-1980s, interest in conservation has waned. Gasoline prices in 1997 were comparable to prices before 1973. Americans are driving more and buying less fuel-efficient cars. Compared to Americans, the Japanese and British use half as much energy per person. Even without conservation, greenhouse gas emissions could be reduced by substituting natural gas for oil and coal. Natural gas, which produces much less pollution than the other fossil fuels, provides one-fifth of the world's energy. Oil, however, is likely to power almost all of the world's more than 600 million vehicles well into the future.

Nuclear and hydroelectric power are the most well-established alternatives to fossil fuels. Both offer a solution to global warming, but not without raising other problems. Nuclear power (which generates 17 percent of the world's electricity) was initially greeted with enthusiasm in the 1950s as a source of clean, inexpensive energy. Nuclear accidents — most notably the explosion within a nuclear power plant in Chernobyl, Ukraine, in 1986 — have focused greater public attention on the dangers of nuclear power. Nonetheless, many countries continue to rely heavily on nuclear energy. France, for example, meets 75 percent of its electricity needs with nuclear power. Hydroelectric power (which supplies 18 percent of the world's electricity) has also encountered mounting opposition in recent decades. As environmentalists emphasize, the dams that are necessary for hydroelectricity choke off rivers and disrupt fragile ecosystems downstream.

Newer renewable energy technologies are safe and environmentally friendly, but have been hobbled by questions of cost and feasibility. Together, they produce less than 1 percent of the world's electricity. Low fossil fuel prices have undercut economic incentives for converting to alternative energy sources. Moreover, the political clout of America's oil, gas, and coal companies has placed fossil fuels at the forefront of U.S. policymaking, while holding back government funding for the development of clean renewable energy. In the last decade, the price of wind power has dropped five times in California. Nonetheless, it remains almost twice as expensive as natural gas for local utilities. The field of solar energy has seen significant advances in the refinement of photovoltaic cells, but few American consumers have adopted the new technology. Photovoltaic cells convert sunlight to electricity. Tens of thousands of solar panels containing the cells are in use in remote areas of Africa, Asia, and Latin America that are not connected to electricity grids. U.S. companies manufacture nearly one-third of the world's solar equipment. With nearly 2 billion people lacking electricity worldwide, they expect their market to boom. Much more experimental is fusion, which produces energy by forcing the nuclei of atoms together. Fusion promises an endless supply of virtually pollution-free power. An international project to build a test reactor, however, is not scheduled for completion until the middle of the 21st century. ❑

For the world's developed countries, industrialization has raised living standards to levels previously unknown in human history. Billions of people in developing countries hope one day to have the lifestyle Americans enjoy. Scientists fear, however, that if the developing world follows the pattern of industrialization pursued by wealthy nations over the past two centuries, the earth will be unable to support the increased level of consumption.

An age of limits

Until recently, concern centered on the depletion of resources. In the 1970s, international panels of scholars and government officials predicted severe food, energy, and raw material shortages before the end of the century. Forecasts of mass starvation were widely accepted.

In fact, many resources have become more plentiful, not less. Since the mid-1970s, the world's recoverable oil reserves have increased by over one-third. U.S. timber harvests are greater than ever, even though America's forests are more extensive than they were in 1920.

Advances in technology have allowed us to break down limits to economic growth. New exploration and extraction techniques have increased supplies of energy and minerals. Manufacturers have learned to substitute plentiful materials for scarce ones and to improve efficiency.

But while technology has enabled humanity to stretch the world's resources further, the problem of pollution poses a more vexing set of limits. America's approach to energy use illustrates the dilemma. If pollution were not a factor, Americans would probably rely much more heavily on our country's vast reserves of coal. Yet growing awareness about the dangers of acid rain and, more recently, global warming have soured America's appetite for coal.

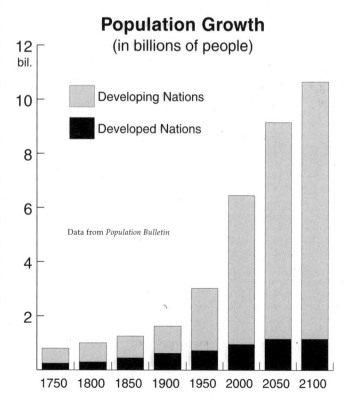

Population Growth
(in billions of people)

Developing Nations

Developed Nations

Data from *Population Bulletin*

Courtesy of Mark Dornblaser

A caribou grazes near an oil pipeline in Alaska.

Even in the area of agricultural development, pollution has raised questions about the price of progress. Since 1960, global food production has more than doubled. Better seeds, greater use of fertilizer, herbicide, and insecticide, the expansion of irrigation, and the introduction of gasoline-powered machinery have helped keep food output ahead of population growth.

At the same time, modern agriculture has contributed its share to higher emissions of greenhouse gases, particularly methane. As farmers worldwide have planted more rice and increased their herds, atmospheric concentrations of methane (which is generated by bacteria in the stomachs of livestock and in the soil of rice paddies) have risen at four times the rate of carbon dioxide and now account for an estimated 12 to 20 percent of global warming.

SECTION 3

Global problems, regional perspectives

Economic and political forces in the 20th century have divided the nations of the world into four broad categories. Each faces a distinct set of environmental challenges and concerns.

The developed world

The developed world produces over half of the world's wealth, consumes most of the world's resources, and generates the bulk of the pollutants that contribute to global warming, ozone depletion, and acid rain. The United States alone accounts for 20 percent of the world's carbon dioxide emissions. Americans, like people throughout the developed world, are particularly dependent on oil. Although the United States is the second leading producer of oil in the world, imports accounted for 44 percent of U.S. oil consumption in 1995.

As the area that industrialized first, the developed world was the first to address the threat of pollution. Developed nations have also been responsible for placing environmental problems on the international agenda.

The former Soviet bloc

The former Soviet bloc suffers from many of the worst features of industrialization. Countries there continue to rely on poor-quality, high-polluting coal and backward, energy-inefficient technologies. In Russia, for example, factories use twice as much energy as their American counterparts for the

Courtesy of Paul Steudler

Economic development has taken a heavy toll in the Amazon region of Brazil.

same output. Russian energy officials estimate that 25 percent of the country's natural gas production is lost to leakage and inefficiency. Meanwhile, energy producers lack the resources to upgrade their equipment.

Nuclear power facilities also pose a serious threat in much of the former Soviet bloc. The Chernobyl accident heightened fears about the fifty-four other reactors in the former Soviet bloc.

Newly industrializing countries

Newly industrializing countries consist mostly of nations in Asia and Latin America that have embarked on economic programs emphasizing rapid industrial development. These countries have turned largely to fossil fuels in order to transform their societies.

China, for example, has become the world's largest producer and consumer of coal. Within twenty-five years, China is expected to overtake the United States and Russia as the leading emitter of greenhouse gases. (Overall, the developing world's share of carbon dioxide emissions is projected to match that of wealthy nations by 2020.) Coal's relative low cost and abundance has made it attractive for China and other poor countries on the road to industrialization, but there is an increasingly heavy price to be paid in the form of polluted skies and acid rain.

In many emerging manufacturing areas, pollution rivals the worst period of industrialization in the United States. In Cairo, the mental development of the city's children has been stunted by pollutants from smelters that extract lead from used car batteries. The number of private cars has shot up in developing nations, but few have fuel-efficiency standards and air quality regulations. Leaders of newly industrializing states argue that they need to keep their farms and factories moving ahead to improve the lives of their people. They want wealthier countries to provide financial assistance to help them install new technologies to reduce greenhouse gas emissions and phase out the use of CFCs.

The underdeveloped world

The underdeveloped world is formed by the poorest countries, located mostly in Africa and South Asia. In these countries, environmental problems are caused less by industrialization than by growing numbers of people relying on the land for food and fuel. Refugees forced onto marginal lands by hunger or civil war inflict the most damage. Deforestation, desertification, and declining biodiversity are widespread in the underdeveloped world.

The famine that struck Somalia in 1992, prompting U.S. troops to intervene to protect international relief efforts, was brought on in part by the Sahel's desertification.

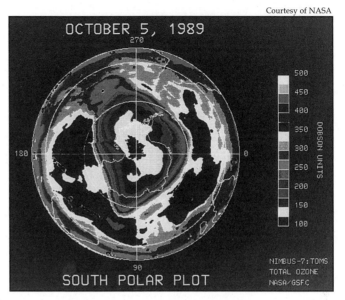

Courtesy of NASA

A satellite photo of ozone depletion over Antarctica.

Because of their often desperate conditions, many underdeveloped countries are more open to far-reaching global programs. Bangladesh, the Maldives islands, and other low-lying countries are particularly concerned that a rise in sea levels brought on by global warming may flood their lands. At the same time, many underdeveloped nations also fear losing control of their natural resources to wealthier countries. For example, underdeveloped countries want a share of the profits from new products derived from species within their borders.

SECTION 4

Green diplomacy

International environmental efforts over the past two decades have often been framed by North-South friction. The dispute is not about the importance of the earth's ecology, but about questions of responsibility and obligation.

Developed nations cite the spiraling population growth rates and the often reckless industrialization of the developing world as the chief threat to the environment. They want poor countries to take stronger measures to curb population growth and address environmental problems.

In contrast, developing nations point the finger at the consumption habits of their affluent counterparts and stress the economic imbalance between the nations of the North and the South. They argue that rich countries should open their markets to more exports from the developing world and absorb the bulk of the costs for helping poor nations meet international pollution standards.

International agreements

The North-South dispute has been played out repeatedly at international conferences on the environment in the 1990s. Most telling is Agenda 21, a diplomatically worded set of guidelines issued by the 1992 Earth Summit after a lengthy negotiating process.

Population growth is hardly mentioned in the 800-page document, due to pressure from developing countries. At the same time, developed nations largely succeeded in keeping out new regulations that would have affected multinational corporations. A new international body, the Commission on Sustainable Development, was created to hold governments accountable for implementing Agenda 21, yet the commission has no enforcement power.

The Earth Summit also produced two legally binding treaties: the Framework Convention on Climate Change and the Convention on Biological Diversity. The United States and other developed countries originally had intended to craft a strong treaty on deforestation that would have banned logging in tropical forests. Many developing countries, however, balked at sacrificing economic growth in the name of environmental protection. India and Malaysia, for example, campaigned against measures that would have regulated their tropical wood industry. Instead, they put forward proposals that logging be restricted in the forests of the developed world. Unable to agree, participants endorsed a vague statement of principles on preserving the world's forests.

Since the Earth Summit, the climate change agreement has dominated the international environmental agenda. By the end of 1997, signatories of the treaty are scheduled to set specific targets for controlling greenhouse gas emissions. The odds for turning back global warming, however, appear poor. Among developed countries, only Switzerland, Britain, and Germany are projected to meet the commitment they made at the Earth Summit to limit greenhouse gas emissions by the year 2000 to 1990 levels. In America's case, emissions are forecast to rise 11 percent during the 1990s. Meanwhile, developing nations have lobbied to be exempted from rigorous emission targets.

International consensus on more narrowly focused environmental goals has proven easier to attain. Agreements on ending the production of ozone-depleting chemicals and curbing ocean pollution are often cited as successes. The challenge, according to international observers, is to strike a balance between economic interests and environmental concerns.

In 1997, for example, the United States and three southern African nations butted heads over the international ban on the sale of ivory. Officials from Botswana, Namibia, and Zimbabwe argued that they should be allowed to sell their stockpiles of ivory, much of which they had confiscated from poachers. They emphasized that their governments had taken effective measures to protect their elephant herds, and that the ivory sales were needed to fund wildlife programs. U.S. representatives contended that easing the ivory ban, even for a few countries, would encourage further poaching.

After lengthy negotiations, members of the Convention on International Trade in Endangered Species agreed to permit Botswana, Namibia, and Zimbabwe to make a limited, one-time sale of ivory to Japan. Although the convention lacks the means to enforce its decisions, poor nations generally comply for fear of losing foreign aid or tourism business from the developed world.

Foreign aid

At the center of the North-South divide is the issue of foreign aid. Organizers of the Earth Summit estimated that $125 billion in aid would be needed annually to implement the conference's recommendations. Meeting that target would require developed countries to increase foreign aid spending by 70 percent.

A number of Western European countries pledged in 1992 to contribute 0.7 percent of their gross domestic product to development assistance by the year 2000. Western Europe's sluggish economy, however, forced most of them to scale back their contributions. Likewise, Americans have shown little enthusiasm for increasing foreign aid spending.

Since the Earth Summit, the dispute over environmentally related foreign aid has been played out primarily in the Global Environment Facility (GEF). Developed countries have donated $2 billion to the GEF to help poor nations meet the standards set at the Earth Summit.

Conflict has revolved around the GEF's decision-making process. Developing countries have long pressed for a larger voice in determining how foreign aid should be spent. Many are especially critical of the World Bank, which has a key administrative role in the GEF. They contend that the World Bank largely represents the interests of the developed world. In hopes of bridging the North-South gulf, GEF member states agreed to a compromise decision-making procedure for allocating aid.

The U.S. position

U.S. environmental policy in the international arena underwent a pronounced shift after the election of Bill Clinton. Under the Bush administration, the U.S. tone at the Earth Summit was often combative. U.S. officials led the developed bloc in arguing that poor countries should do more to help themselves. For example, they criticized governments in the developing world for providing electricity and irrigation water at cut-rate prices. Selling natural resources too cheaply, they asserted, encouraged inefficiency, waste, and pollution. The United States also lobbied to weaken the Earth Summit's climate change treaty and refused to sign the biodiversity treaty. Bush feared that the biodiversity treaty would allow foreign countries to claim a share of the profits and technology of U.S. biotechnology companies.

After coming to office, Clinton signed the climate change and biodiversity treaties, and contributed $430 million to the GEF. In 1997, Clinton recognized the threat posed by global warming and pledged U.S. support for establishing binding targets for the reduction of greenhouse gas emissions. The president, however, resisted firm timetables. In contrast, his Western European counterparts proposed cutting emissions by 15 percent from 1990 levels by 2010.

SECTION 5 ———————————————————

Views on U.S. options

Now that you have read about some of the issues related to U.S. policy on global environmental problems, it is time to take a closer look at what our country's position should be. In this section, you will explore four views on U.S. global environmental policy. As you will see, each of the views is based on a distinct set of values and beliefs, and is shaped by a well-defined perspective on the threats and opportunities facing the United States.

The views presented address three fundamental questions that frame the discussion on U.S. policy toward global environmental problems:

•**How significant are the threats posed by environmental degradation?** Should the potential long-term gravity of global warming, ozone depletion, and other environmental problems give them priority over other concerns? Or should global environmental problems rank below those economic issues that have a more immediate impact on the lives of Americans?

•**Which parts of the world pose the greatest threats to the global environment?** Should the United States and other developed countries accept responsibility for contributing most to global environmental problems and take steps to reduce consumption? Or should the developed world concentrate on pressuring developing countries to curb population growth and establish strict measures to reduce pollution?

•**What should be our relationship to the international community regarding global environmental problems?** Should the United States be willing to give up some of its sovereignty to international organizations to establish global environmental standards? Or should the United States chart its own course on environmental policy and guard against efforts to extend the authority of the UN?

Each of the four views that follows responds differently to these questions. You should think of the views as a tool designed to help you examine the contrasting strategies from which Americans must define our country's role in the world and craft future policy.

View 1 — Put the economy first

Global environmental problems should take a back seat to invigorating the U.S. economy. That's what really touches the lives of Americans today. At a time when the United States is locked in an intense struggle for global economic competitiveness, we cannot afford environmental policies that will hamstring our economy and cost American jobs. The livelihoods of American workers should not be sacrificed in the name of a distant and uncertain threat, particularly while scientists continue to debate the meaning of ambiguous research data.

Considering trade-offs

•Will neglecting environmental problems in the name of economic growth result in still greater harm to the health of both future generations and the planet as a whole?

•Will refusing to work with the UN on global environmental issues leave the United States isolated in the international community?

•Will giving environmental problems a low priority cause U.S. science and industry to fall behind in an expanding field?

View 2 — Take the lead

We should take the lead in developing environmentally friendly technologies that strengthen our economy. Faced with competition from Western Europe and Japan, the United States cannot afford to lag behind in this expanding field. To accomplish our goals, the United States should avoid becoming entangled in the endless debates and discussions of international organizations. By acting decisively, not only do we provide a cleaner world for future generations of Americans, but we also ensure that the United States remains on the cutting edge of science and industry.

Considering trade-offs

• Will charting our own course on environmental policies offend our key allies and spark resentment in developing countries?

• Will the absence of a cooperative international approach to the environment exacerbate global problems, such as the decline of biodiversity?

• Will investing tax dollars in unproven environmental technologies deprive other emerging industries of capital and increase the budget deficit?

View 3 — Share environmental responsibility

Despite the progress of wealthy nations in curbing pollution, the developing world's rapid population growth and irresponsible development continues to pose a mounting threat to the planet. Isolating ourselves from damage to the environment is not possible. In the end, only the developed countries have the technological know-how and the economic strength to restore the health of the planet. In cooperation with other developed nations, we should address the problems that lead to environmental destruction and oversee programs to implement environmentally responsible policies in poor countries.

Considering trade-offs

• Will poor countries refuse to cooperate if the developed world takes the lead in setting global environmental policies that hamper their development?

• Will increased spending on international environmental programs siphon resources away from addressing pressing problems here at home?

• Will the bureaucracy and regulations required to coordinate international environmental efforts stifle the growth of U.S. businesses, especially in the field of environmental technologies?

View 4 — Promote global stewardship

With the survival of the planet at stake, global environmental problems outweigh national interests and must rank as the top priority on our national agenda. As Americans, we must recognize that we are responsible for more than our share of pollution, and we should channel our technological resources toward creating a global economy that is environmentally sustainable for generations to come. The common good of the planet requires that we be willing to give up some of our sovereignty to international organizations and embrace countries of the developing world as partners in global decision-making on environmental issues.

Considering trade-offs

• Will greatly expanding the power of international organizations to govern the environment mean giving up authority to manage our country's land, water, and air?

• Will giving poor countries broader international influence and additional economic aid foster still greater corruption and inefficiency in the developing world, while doing little to improve the environment?

• Will stringent new regulations and big increases in government spending drag down the U.S. economy?

Your turn

These views are by no means the only U.S. options. Rather, they are intended to lay out some of the most important values and assumptions underlying the debate on U.S. environmental policy and to spur discussion on the direction our country should take regarding this pressing issue. When you meet next time, you will have an opportunity to discuss U.S. environmental policy with others. The following statements are designed to help you clarify your thoughts on what is most important to you concerning this issue. Take a few moments to respond. This is a tool for you to get started. It will not be collected.

Rate each of the statements according to your beliefs:

1 = Strongly Support	3 = Oppose	5 = Undecided
2 = Support	4 = Strongly Oppose	

___ The interests of the United States can be maintained only if we resolutely exercise our power and influence in international affairs.

___ Americans today need to make sacrifices in their way of life to safeguard the world for future generations.

___ Problems in the international arena are far less important for Americans than the challenges we face at home, such as poverty, crime, and budget deficits.

___ Countries that are poor and technologically backward have only themselves to blame.

___ The United States should recognize that problems in the developing world, such as poverty and environmental degradation, must be addressed as problems that affect everyone on the planet.

___ In our competitive world, the United States cannot afford to give up any advantage in science and technology.

___ To solve global environmental problems, rich and poor countries must work together.

___ The health of the U.S. economy has a greater impact on the lives of Americans than any other issue.

___ The United States should be willing to give up some of its own sovereignty to promote international cooperation.

___ The United States cannot afford to give other nations a say in policies by which Americans must live.

Suggested reading

Black, Michael and Fischer, Frank, eds. *Greening Environmental Policy: The Politics of a Sustainable Future* (New York: St. Martin's Press, 1995).

Bolch, Ben and Lyons, Harold. *Apocalypse Not: Science, Economics, and Environmentalism* (Washington, D.C.: Cato Institute, 1993).

Easterbrook, Gregg. *A Moment on the Earth: The Coming Age of Environmental Optimism* (New York: Viking Press, 1995).

Silver, Cheryl Simon and DeFries, Ruth S. *One Earth One Future: Our Changing Global Environment* (Washington, D.C.: National Academy Press, 1990).

Chapter 5

U.S. Trade Policy: Competing in a Global Economy

By the mid-1990s, the U.S. economy was cruising in high gear. Unemployment was down below 5 percent. Inflation held steady at around 3 percent annually. The gross domestic product (GDP) was growing at an impressive clip. The stock market soared to record heights and corporate profits were stronger than ever. The confidence of American consumers stood at an all-time high.

Americans had good cause to be bullish about their country's economy. After years of corporate downsizing, productivity improvements, and government budget cuts, the U.S. economy had emerged leaner and fitter. Economists lauded the United States for leading the developed world in adjusting to the demands of economic globalization. American companies were again at the forefront of cutting-edge technologies and industries of the future.

Yet beneath the statistics and the analyses, the pressures of globalization continue to recast the economic landscape and unsettle the lives of

Foundations of the International Trading System

For its first century and a half, the United States shielded fledgling manufacturing industries from foreign competition while assertively seeking out new markets overseas. U.S. import tariffs remained above 30 percent (as compared to under 3 percent today) throughout most of the 19th century. U.S. leaders felt at the time that the country's economy would require decades of protectionist measures to catch up with British industry and consequently saw few benefits in free trade.

World War II dramatically altered the American worldview. At the close of the war, George Kennan, the architect of the U.S. strategy for containing the Soviet Union, maintained that there were five centers of industrial and military power: the United States, the Soviet Union, Britain, Germany and central Europe, and Japan. To stop Soviet expansion, Kennan held that the

United States needed to ensure that the other three powers were pro-American and economically strong. President Harry Truman and his successors followed Kennan's recommendations.

Leaders of Truman's generation believed that free trade was crucial to the health of the U.S. economy and the stability of the West. They recalled that an increase of U.S. import tariffs in 1930 had cut American trade in half, exacerbating the Depression and further weakening the international economy. Truman's top priority was to restore the prosperity of American trading partners in Western Europe. The key element in promoting Western Europe's recovery was the Marshall Plan. From 1948 to 1952, the United States supplied $12.5 billion (equivalent to about $85 billion in 1997 dollars) in aid to the region.

To lower trade barriers in the noncommunist world, the United States pressed for

millions of Americans. Each year, a greater share of the U.S. economy becomes linked to foreign trade. Transnational corporations are blurring the distinction between imports and exports. American businesses and workers are increasingly forced to compete in a global marketplace. Many of America's flagship corporations are moving factories and jobs overseas. Others are entering joint ventures or negotiating mergers with foreign companies.

For the moment, the United States seems to have turned the forces of change to its advantage. Our society's enthusiasm for innovation and technology has spawned companies that can shift gears at a moment's notice. Economic globalization has opened up a world of opportunity for U.S. exporters. American consumers are able to choose from a cornucopia of imports, and millions of investors are reaping the rewards of the liberalized international capital market.

But the turmoil has left our country uneasy. Even as they profess optimism about their economic prospects, Americans understand that the

the establishment of the General Agreement on Tariffs and Trade (GATT). GATT hastened the trend toward a global trading system by laying out a set of ground rules among the twenty-three original members. From GATT's founding session in Geneva, when import tariffs worldwide averaged about 40 percent, the United States carried the banner of free trade through six additional rounds of negotiations.

As trade barriers fell, world trade increased from $53 billion in 1948 to nearly $1.5 trillion in the mid-1970s, to more than $6.3 trillion today. American exports soared and access to the American market helped key U.S. allies recover from World War II. By 1986, when the eighth round of GATT talks convened in Uruguay, import tariffs worldwide had fallen to roughly 5 percent.

The United States also encouraged trading partnerships in Western Europe and East Asia. In 1957, the six-nation European Economic Community emerged. The trading bloc (known today as the European Union) eliminated many restrictions on the movement of people, goods, services, and capital among member nations. Today, the European Union (EU) represents an economy larger than that of the United States.

In East Asia, U.S. policies helped make Japan a regional hub of economic activity. As the Japanese economy took off, it developed close economic ties with important U.S. allies in the region. The success of East Asia's "four tigers" — South Korea, Taiwan, Hong Kong, and Singapore — was part of a larger U.S. effort to strengthen countries on the front line of the struggle against communism. High import tariffs, relative to U.S. levels, were used in both Western Europe and East Asia to protect key local industries. ❏

security and stability of the past have been swept away. Businesses large and small must learn to compete on a global scale or be left by the wayside. Wages for millions of American workers are being held down by the constraints of the international labor market. The demands of global financial institutions often dictate national fiscal policy.

In the midst of such upheaval, it is not surprising that the debate on U.S. trade policy is riddled with contradictions and paradoxes. The issues on the U.S. trade agenda demand that we think through our country's place in the global economy and sort out our national priorities.

Should tariffs be raised to protect the American economy from foreign competition, or should they be kept low to provide a wide selection of consumer goods and to promote innovation among American industries? Should the government provide select industries an edge in the global marketplace, or should market forces determine success and failure? And what of the connection between international trade and foreign policy issues? Should we be using trade policy as a tool in promoting human rights and democracy? Should trade benefits be awarded to countries that embrace American political values? This chapter will help prepare you to consider these questions.

Changing U.S. Export Patterns

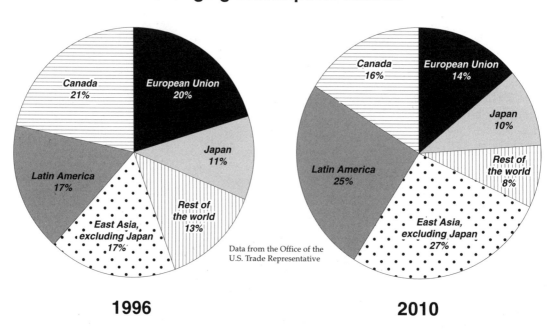

Data from the Office of the U.S. Trade Representative

1996   **2010**

SECTION 1

Global economic pressures

As we approach the 21st century, the U.S. economy remains the world's largest — over twice the size of our nearest competitor, Japan. The U.S. dollar serves as the accepted currency of international trade. In 1996, the United States led the world in exports. The United States also maintains a lead in many of the future's most promising industries, including biotechnology, telecommunications, and environmentally friendly products.

However, the United States no longer dominates the world economy as it did in 1950. At that time, U.S. manufacturing output accounted for roughly half of the world total (compared to slightly over one-fifth today). Americans have watched their automobile, steel, and consumer electronics industries lose ground to foreign competition. Whereas in 1950 countries throughout the world turned to the United States as a source of capital, today the United States is the world's biggest borrower. Budget deficits have forced the United States to rely on foreign lenders to finance government spending. In addition, the United States now suffers chronic trade deficits instead of the trade surpluses routinely recorded in the 1950s and 1960s.

The relative change of the U.S. position in the international economy does not mean that the United States has become poorer. On the contrary, U.S. per capita income has continued to increase even as countries in Western Europe and Japan have caught up economically with the United States. What has changed is the nature of the global economy. Goods and services now cross borders at an ever more rapid pace, and the market for labor and capital has acquired an increasingly global character. U.S. corporations have sought a competitive edge by taking advantage of cheap labor in Latin America and Asia. Meanwhile, Japanese and Western European companies have invested in the United States, hoping to benefit from American research expertise and to tap the huge American market.

On a still larger scale, the global balance of economic strength is shifting from the developed world to the developing world. Developed countries, which in 1994 accounted for 56 percent of world economic production, will see their share of global output drop to below 40 percent by 2020. In turn, developing nations, particularly those in East Asia, will continue to surge forward. China's GDP is likely to surpass that of the United States in the next two decades.

Winners and losers

Ultimately, the question of the U.S. economy's health hinges on perspective. Many economists view the 1980s as a pivotal decade, when American firms improved their efficiency and U.S. exports began expanding. In many high-tech fields, ranging from microelectronics to telecommunications equipment, the United States has widened its lead in global exports during the last decade. A growing share of U.S. exports are generated by a vibrant service sector that employs Americans in industries ranging from business insurance to computer software to international hotel management. American workers have recorded strong gains in productivity too, especially as the economy emerged from the 1990-91 recession. Overall, the opening of new markets has proved to be a boon for American industry. Most business executives, especially those in export-oriented areas, are optimistic regarding the United States' ability to compete globally.

The growth in trade has also given American consumers a wider range of products to buy. The increased competition has forced producers to improve quality and hold down prices. Low-income Americans, who spend a larger share of their money on consumer goods, have been among the prime beneficiaries of lower prices.

But while U.S. trade opportunities have expanded and new consumer goods have entered the market, most American manufacturing workers have not welcomed competition on a worldwide scale. They fear that the forces of open trade threaten their way of life. Statistics suggest that they have cause for concern. From 1979 to 1995, U.S. industrial output doubled, and yet wages fell. Roughly 3 million manufacturing jobs were lost in the United States during the period. As the share of workers with health and pension benefits declines, economists

calculate that Americans in the labor force under 30 will earn less than their parents in their lifetimes.

In 1995, after four years of economic expansion, the income of an average American household rose for the first time since 1989. Over the past decade, the gap between rich and poor in our country has widened. In 1995, the top fifth of American households earned 48.7 percent of the nation's income, while the bottom fifth earned just 3.7 percent.

In the quest to hone economic competitiveness, the United States has taken the most dramatic steps in the developed world. Both Republicans and Democrats have embraced the cause of trimming the welfare state and lowering the federal budget deficit. In the private sector, business executives have been rewarded for squeezing worker benefits and holding down wages. As a result, the American economy by 1997 was moving along a significantly different track than the economies of Western Europe. Whereas the American economic model was characterized by high growth, low unemployment, stagnant wages, and often jarring change, Western Europe was wedded to maintaining job security and stability, even as performance sputtered. During the 1990s, the U.S. economy has generated nearly 12 million new jobs and pushed unemployment below 5 percent, while the jobless rate in Western Europe has hovered around 12 percent.

A Role for Government?

While wrestling over international trade issues, Clinton administration officials have been attracted to the government-industry partnerships prevalent among many of America's trading partners. The president, for example, has called for cooperation between Washington and business to develop a new generation of fuel-efficient cars and to spur advances in information technologies. In suggesting that the United States pursue an industrial policy to gain a competitive edge, Clinton's advisers are reviving a notion that had been articulated by Alexander Hamilton two centuries earlier.

In the 19th century, Hamilton's recommendations were put into practice. Government contracts, especially for the armed forces, were aimed at stimulating strategic sectors of manufacturing, while nascent industries were protected by an import tariff that hovered around 30 percent.

World War II and the Cold War prompted government-industry partnerships in the name of national security. In the 1970s, the U.S. government promoted the development of synthetic fuels to lessen the country's dependence on imported oil. The energy industry, however, lost its enthusiasm for the project after oil prices began falling in the 1980s. Other examples of government-industry cooperation were more successful. In 1987, the government teamed up with a consortium of American computer chip makers to explore high-risk areas of research, and to open communication channels between computer chip manufacturers and suppliers of manufacturing equipment. The results of this effort, known as Sematech, were credited in part with reversing the decline of the American computer chip industry. Hailing Sematech as a model for government-industry cooperation, Clinton administration officials have claimed that the approach can be applied to their plans to develop more fuel-efficient cars. Other industry consortia, including groups of aerospace and textile manufacturers, have lobbied for similar government assistance.

Meanwhile in Japan, officials have had second thoughts about the viability of government efforts to strengthen Japan's economic position in world markets. The system of government planning that helped make Japan's automobile and electronics industries world leaders has been less successful in high-technology fields. In the early 1980s, for example, Japanese government and industry joined forces to spur forward the computer industry. The project, however, was not nimble enough to keep pace with the rapid advances generated by small computer companies.

Among Americans, the Japanese experience has produced contradictory interpretations. For those who admire Japan's industrial policy, Japanese government-industry cooperation offers lessons that Americans should consider. They argue that, as in Japan, the U.S. concept of national security should include a commitment to the viability of critical industries, such as aviation and computers. Critics, however, insist that the involvement of government is often a negative force. They maintain that Washington inevitably favors large corporations with political influence, and stifles initiative and innovation. ❏

SECTION 2

Redefining trade relations

With the Cold War over, the national security priorities that guided U.S. trade policy and the alliance system that bound the United States to its trading partners in Western Europe and Japan have lost much of their significance. U.S. trade interests seem to be pointing in new directions. In the next twenty-five years, for example, developing countries are likely to account for about two-thirds of the increase in world imports. America's exports to the countries of the developing world and the former Soviet bloc, which already represent 40 percent of total U.S. exports, are expected to rise sharply.

U.S. leaders have attempted to keep pace with the future by actively promoting new trade ties. Their most notable achievements have been the World Trade Organization (WTO) and the North American Free Trade Agreement (NAFTA). The WTO and NAFTA are both designed to reduce barriers to international trade. The scope of the WTO (previously known as the General Agreement on Tariffs and Trade) is worldwide, with a membership of more than 130 nations by 1997, while NAFTA is limited to the United States, Mexico, and Canada.

More than any previous trade agreements, NAFTA and the WTO have pushed news about trade policy from the business section to the front page. The congressional debate on NAFTA in the fall of 1993 — followed a year later by the vote on the WTO — drew the heavyweights of business and labor into the ring, and captured the national spotlight for weeks. Not since the Civil War, when the industrial North and the agricultural South squared off in Congress over import tariffs, had trade issues generated such intense interest.

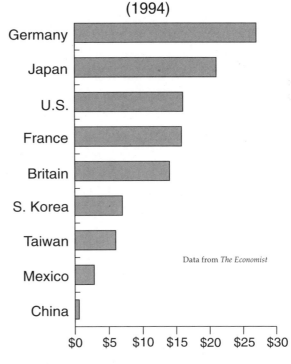

Labor Costs in Manufacturing
(1994)

Data from *The Economist*

Wages and benefits per hour

The WTO and NAFTA

The latest round of WTO talks was concluded in 1993 after seven years of negotiations. Free trade advocates were generally pleased that services had been on the agenda for the first time and that the accord produced a major breakthrough in agriculture. The agreement also required participating countries to lower tariffs and respect copyright laws on computer software, music, and other intellectual property. However, several of the thorniest issues — including entertainment and financial services — were not included in the agreement.

Trade specialists are already looking ahead to a further expansion of the WTO. The next round of talks will probably reconsider services. A more sensitive issue is removing non-tariff barriers to trade — an area of special interest to the United States. Over the years, non-tariff barriers have risen worldwide even as the WTO has lowered import tariffs. Some non-tariff barriers are fair. Virtually every country, for example, regulates trade to protect the health and safety of its citizens. In some cases, however, these rules have been crafted to discriminate against imports. American companies often complain that the close relationship between Japanese manufacturers and Japanese retailers effectively keeps American exports out of stores in Japan. Many governments also reinforce non-tariff barriers by favoring local companies in their purchasing decisions.

The approval of NAFTA marked a departure from the strategy that has driven U.S. involvement in the WTO. Unlike the global scope of the WTO, NAFTA is limited to North America. The goals of NAFTA, however, are much more ambitious than those of the WTO. The WTO sets rules to promote more open trade, while NAFTA aims to eliminate trade barriers entirely. The agreement represents an acknowledgment by American leaders that the United States, like the countries of the EU, is better off in a regional trading bloc. Canada has long been our country's leading trade partner, while Mexico ranks third behind Canada and Japan.

Trade analysts see NAFTA as a source of leverage for the United States in dealing with the countries of the EU and East Asia. NAFTA's most lasting impact, however, may have more to do with our country's changing relationship with Mexico. NAFTA marks a bold attempt to bridge the wide economic gulf between the developed nations of the United States and Canada and the developing economy of Mexico.

Since NAFTA's implementation, the United States and Mexico have already weathered one financial storm together. In December 1994, confidence in the

Mexican peso suddenly collapsed. Within a few weeks, the currency lost nearly half its value against the dollar. To help stabilize the peso, President Clinton came forward with a $12.5 billion loan. His response left little doubt that NAFTA had increased Washington's stake in the health of the Mexican economy.

The U.S.-Mexican trade picture reflects the peso's gyrations. During NAFTA's first year, trade between the two neighbors rose over 20 percent and the United States recorded a surplus. The fall of the peso, however, was accompanied by a sharp drop in Mexican imports. Imports have gradually recovered since the financial crisis, but the U.S.-Mexican balance of trade has remained tilted in favor of Mexico.

New partnerships

U.S. participation in the WTO and NAFTA will come up for review periodically in the next few years. Meanwhile, the discussion about U.S. trade policy has already moved beyond the current agreements to the possibility of creating a huge new trading bloc involving countries of the Pacific Rim and broadening NAFTA to incorporate the entire Western Hemisphere.

Tom Toles copyright 1986 *The Buffalo News*. Reprinted with permission of UPS. All rights reserved.

The initiative in the Pacific Rim revolves around the Asia-Pacific Economic Cooperation (APEC) group. In 1993, Clinton convened the first summit of APEC's eighteen member states and nudged the group toward forming a regional trading bloc. In 1995, APEC members agreed to voluntary guidelines for establishing a free-trade zone. Developed countries would be expected to lower their trade barriers by 2010, while developing nations would be given until 2020.

The potential of a Pacific Rim free-trade zone is indeed tantalizing. The APEC countries, which include China, South Korea, and other booming East Asian economies, are home to more than 2 billion people and account for more than half the world's output. The road to an APEC trade pact, however, promises to be bumpy. The United States and Australia have been the strongest advocates of free trade within the group. In contrast, many of APEC's East Asian members have achieved robust economic growth while maintaining high tariffs and other protectionist measures. Most observers believe that APEC is decades away from achieving the tightly knit integration of the fifteen-nation EU.

Progress on the southward expansion of NAFTA is likely to come much sooner. In 1994, thirty-four leaders of countries in the Western Hemisphere approved a declaration calling for the formation of a free-trade area in the Americas by 2005. Chile, which is hailed by free-trade advocates as a model of economic reform, is considered first in line to be included in NAFTA. There are also proposals to combine features of NAFTA with those of other regional trade pacts, such as the Mercosur union of Brazil, Argentina, Uruguay, and Paraguay.

Voices of opposition

The fanfare of economic summits and trade accords has not quieted the debate on the direction of U.S. trade policy. On the contrary, trade policy has become a lightning rod for the larger controversy surrounding economic globalization. Critics of free trade contend that a wealthy elite has

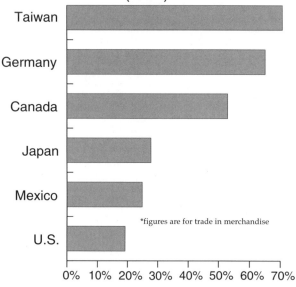

Trade* as a Percentage of GDP
(1996)

Taiwan
Germany
Canada
Japan
Mexico
U.S.

*figures are for trade in merchandise

0% 10% 20% 30% 40% 50% 60% 70%

reaped most of the rewards of globalization. In their view, the big winners are transnational corporations that take advantage of cheaper labor costs in Mexico and other countries of the developing world. Free trade critics claim that the majority of Americans have suffered from heightened global competition. They are particularly concerned about the fate of unskilled workers who are least able to cope with economic change.

As the debate has heated up, progress toward extending NAFTA, formalizing APEC, and expanding the scope of the WTO has bogged down. Key figures in both the Republican and Democratic parties have balked at giving President Clinton "fast-track" authority to negotiate new trade agreements. (Under the fast-track provision, Congress is required to either approve or reject new agreements, but cannot offer amendments.) Several prospective candidates for the next presidential election clearly view trade as a hot-button issue and have already staked out firm positions.

In fact, the economic impact of recent trade accords has been much less dramatic than the political rhetoric would suggest. NAFTA, for example, has caused barely a ripple in the overall U.S. employment picture. According to a Clinton administration study released in 1997, the first three years of NAFTA generated, at most, 160,000 new jobs, while displacing no more than 100,000 workers.

Critics of free trade see the trade agreements as a broader threat to American society. They warn that the agreements put pressure on the United States to weaken its standards on environmental protection and worker safety. The WTO has become one of their favorite targets. As intended, the newly created body has put teeth in the rules that govern global trade. Under the General Agreement on Tariffs and Trade (GATT), each participating country had the power to veto GATT decisions. The WTO has eliminated veto power. Instead, member states are obliged to comply with WTO rulings in international trade disputes.

For opponents of the WTO, the fear is that the authority of international bureaucrats will increase at the expense of U.S. sovereignty. Environmentalists, labor union leaders, and consumer advocates argue that foreign countries will use the WTO to attack U.S. regulations as unfair trade barriers. Laws intended to protect the environment, workers' rights, and the health and safety of consumers could be especially vulnerable.

The WTO's first major ruling in an international dispute gave critics reason for concern. The case was brought by Venezuela and Brazil, which charged that imported gasoline was held to a stricter standard for emissions in some instances than gasoline produced by American companies. In 1996, the WTO determined that provisions of the U.S. Clean Air Act discriminated against foreign refiners of gasoline. At the same time, the WTO acknowledged that the United States had the right to enforce laws combatting air pollution.

Before approving the WTO pact in 1994, the U.S. Senate insisted that President Clinton form a panel of judges to review WTO decisions. If the panel finds that the United States has been subjected to three unfair rulings over a five-year period, Congress could vote for U.S. withdrawal from the trade agreement.

The foreign policy connection

The trade debate also continues to spill over into the realm of post-Cold War foreign policy. With respect to the developing world, trade policy has often been viewed as a tool for promoting democracy, human rights, and environmental protection.

Much of the debate has centered on China, the fourth-largest U.S. trading partner in recent years. Critics of China's policies have favored withdrawing Beijing's most-favored-nation status (which allows countries to import goods to the United States at the lowest tariff rates) to convince China to change its ways regarding the use of prison labor, the persecution of political dissidents, the repression of Tibetan culture, and other human rights issues.

President Clinton, however, has backed away from his earlier commitment to link U.S.-Chinese trade with Beijing's human rights record. Instead, the Clinton administration has concentrated on pressing China to crack down on pirate factories that ignore intellectual property rights protecting computer software, music, and other products.

Meanwhile, trade disputes between the United States and its partners in the developed world have continued to gain attention. American trade relations with Japan are a long-standing sore point. Our country's trade deficit with Japan totaled $48 billion in 1996, larger than the U.S. deficit with any other country. Under President Clinton, the United States has taken a more assertive tone toward Japan. Clinton has pushed the Japanese leadership to boost consumer demand for American goods. Japan's imports from the United States have increased in recent years, but Tokyo has sidestepped efforts to set specific targets for reducing Japan's trade surplus with the United States.

Steve Sack. Reprinted with permission. Tribune Media Services.

How trade affects us

Advocates on all sides of the trade policy debate often seek to personalize the abstractions of international commerce. The individual profiles that follow go beyond the details of specific trade agreements to consider how trade policy relates to the lives of four Americans. Although the characters are not real, their hopes and concerns typify attitudes found throughout the country.

Profile # 1

Judy lives in a New England city with a long industrial history. Like many people in her neighborhood, she works in a jewelry factory assembling earrings and necklaces. She is a high school graduate, but with three children to raise Judy has not found the time for further education. Along with many of her co-workers, Judy is worried about the future of her job.

Judy, now in her mid-40s, has worked in the same non-union factory for twelve years. During that time, her salary has barely kept up with inflation. In 1997, she was making $7.75 an hour. Judy's employer offers a health plan, but since the late 1980s benefits have been steadily reduced while the contribution required from employees has increased. Although Judy would like to find a better job, she considers herself lucky to have steady work, as there have been a number of layoffs in her factory. Two years ago, a nearby jewelry factory closed down when manufacturing operations moved to Malaysia.

Judy has come to recognize that her factory is competing against low-wage countries in Latin America and Asia. For her, free trade represents a threat. She realizes that some American businesses will benefit from more open markets, but feels that American workers have little to gain.

The trends of the past two decades justify Judy's concerns. Since 1979, the proportion of full-time working people unable to earn enough to keep their families above the poverty line has increased by 50 percent. The 70 million American workers who, like Judy, are classified as unskilled have found themselves competing with workers in developing countries for jobs. Global economic pressures have also encouraged many companies to reduce their work forces. The largest cuts in the 1990s have come from the giants of American industry. General Motors, for example, has laid off 70,000 workers, while IBM has slashed 63,000 jobs. Even after a year of healthy profits, AT&T announced in early 1996 that it would eliminate 40,000 jobs over the next three years.

As free trade expands, workers like Judy face greater competition from their counterparts in developing countries. Wages in Mexico, for example, average one-sixth of U.S. levels. Although the average Mexican worker has only a sixth-grade education, productivity in some factories is equal to U.S. standards. Under NAFTA, more companies are expected to take advantage of Mexico's cheap labor costs and easy access to the American market.

The effect of the 1989 U.S.-Canadian free trade pact also seems to justify Judy's concern. Labor unions have traditionally been stronger in Canada than in the United States and employers have paid more in taxes for unemployment insurance. As a result, the free trade agreement put some Canadian companies at a competitive disadvantage. From 1989 to 1992, the output of Canada's factories fell 11.4 percent, compared to a 1.6 percent gain in the United States, and employment in Canadian manufacturing fell by 15 percent.

Judy wants the protection of American jobs to be the top priority of U.S. trade policy. She also hopes that the government will help workers adjust to the impact of changing trade patterns. She believes training workers in new job skills would be helpful. The government, she feels, should encourage companies to invest more in the education of their workers. Firms in Germany, Japan, and other developed nations are well ahead of the United States in worker training. Furthermore, many students in these countries finish their high school education by taking part in advanced apprenticeship programs. Judy would like to see such opportunities for her children.

Profile #2

Vicky lives in Atlanta, the city that has been her home since she found a job there as a sales representative for a telecommunications firm. Vicky, who will soon be 30 years old, has had a strong interest in international business since high school. In her senior year, she served as an intern at a company that sold aviation equipment to East Asia. In college, Vicky spent a year in Taiwan on a student exchange program. Her experience abroad led Vicky to change her major to international marketing.

Since graduating, Vicky has worked for three different telecommunications companies. At her current job, Vicky is part of a division that markets cellular telephones to businesses. Her division has increasingly found customers in the Caribbean and Latin America, where poor telephone service makes cellular communications an appealing option. The Mexican market, once heavily protected, has seen the highest rates of growth. Opportunities in Mexico began to open in 1990, when the government sold the state-run communications monopoly, *Teléfonos de México*, to private investors.

Under NAFTA, the barriers that have shielded Mexico's telecommunications industry are being lowered further, and Vicky's company is well-positioned to widen its customer base. In Mexico City, for example, thousands of businesses already rely on cellular telephones as an alternative to *Teléfonos de México*.

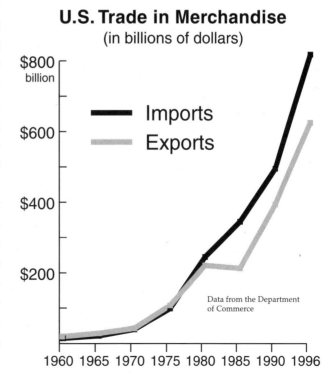

U.S. Trade in Merchandise
(in billions of dollars)

Data from the Department of Commerce

By promptly connecting new accounts and offering a variety of service packages, Vicky's company hopes to capture a sizable share of the Mexican market.

In the next few years, company executives also hope to gain a foothold in China. Vicky would be a key part of her company's operations. Not only does she speak Chinese, but Vicky has acquired international business experience through her previous jobs. China's leaders, however, have tightly limited the sphere of foreign investment, and their country has yet to be admitted into the WTO. China has been particularly slow in opening its economy to foreign companies that specialize in business services, such as Vicky's firm.

Assuming trade barriers fall in China and other countries, American companies that provide business services such as banking, insurance, advertising, and telecommunications are ready to take advantage of new opportunities. The ethnic and cultural diversity of the United States, along with the worldwide acceptance of American business standards, should give Americans a competitive edge.

Economists note that the United States has shifted away from manufacturing bulky goods and moved toward a high-technology, information-oriented economy. When services are taken into account, the U.S. trade picture brightens considerably. In 1996, for example, the United States imported $191 billion more in merchandise than it exported. At the same time, the United States enjoyed a $80 billion trade surplus in services. American exports of commercial services consistently have led the world, typically doubling the total of the United States' nearest competitor. More open trade is expected to give an added boost to the service sector.

Profile #3

Al lives in a small Midwestern city that has been dominated by the automobile industry for most of this century. When Al was growing up, Al's relatives and neighbors worked either in the General Motors (GM) factory or in one of the smaller plants that supplied auto parts. Al always figured that he too would end up working in the auto industry. In college, he earned an engineering degree, and then went to work for the local GM plant. After ten years with GM, Al and two of his fellow engineers opened a factory that produces gaskets for the engines of GM cars. Now in his late 50s, Al employs more than 100 people and supplies gaskets to GM, Ford, and Toyota factories in the United States and Mexico.

When Al opened his plant, American companies were still the unquestioned leaders of the auto industry. Most of his business, as well as his competition, could be found within a few hundred miles of his home. In the last two decades, companies in Japan and South Korea have entered the U.S. market with greater force, creating a more competitive and global business environment. In 1995, for example, Japanese companies manufactured nearly 1.8 million vehicles in their American plants. To meet the changing demands of the market, Al has hired more engineers to design new gaskets. He also has streamlined his manufacturing operation to the point where he produces gaskets only for specific orders. This has allowed him to trim his manufacturing costs, and to avoid maintenance expenses for overstocked warehouses.

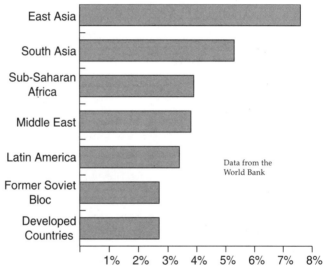

Projected Economic Growth Rates
(1994-2003)

Data from the World Bank

Annual increase in GDP

Al knows his competition in East Asia also continues to raise productivity levels. From 1973 to 1989, the productivity of Japanese workers increased by 5.5 percent annually, compared to a 2.6 percent yearly rise in the United States. Wage costs also concern Al. Full-time workers in Al's factory earn $13 an hour and receive health insurance. Mexican workers performing the same jobs earn about $2 an hour. That gap in wages has Al worried about NAFTA. A number of companies that compete with him set up plants in Mexico in the 1980s. With the approval of NAFTA, others have followed.

There is also a positive side to NAFTA for Al. Mexico is one of the fastest-growing automobile markets in the world and has contributed to the recent rebound of the U.S. automobile industry. Al has seen his exports to Mexico triple since 1986, the year when Mexico began a sweeping economic liberalization program. He is part of a trade boom that saw U.S. exports of auto parts to Mexico increase by about 65 percent from 1991 to 1994. Under NAFTA, Mexico's tariffs on cars and light trucks have been cut in half, and tariffs on most auto parts coming into Mexico will be eliminated by the end of the century. The Mexican market for new vehicles is forecast to grow by at least 65 percent between 1994 and 2000.

American manufacturers such as Al have reason to be optimistic about broader trends in global trade. From 1992 to 1996, U.S. exports rose 27 percent. About half of U.S. economic growth during the period was tied to exports. Economists note that global competition has forced American companies to improve quality and hold down costs. Even in well-established U.S. export industries — such as agriculture, electrical machinery, aviation, and computer equipment — continued innovation has boosted American competitiveness.

Profile #4

Gerald is a design engineer with an aviation manufacturer in Southern California. For twenty-five years, Gerald has been designing fighter planes for the U.S. Air Force and several of our country's allies abroad. With his 65th birthday less than two years away, Gerald is ambivalent about the prospect of retirement.

Gerald and his wife, Teresa, have lived comfortably in a Los Angeles suburb for over two decades. Their two children graduated from California universities and have moved out on their own. Every summer the couple visits Mexico, Teresa's native country.

During the 1980s, it was difficult to find a more secure job than Gerald's. Production in the aviation industry, buoyed by a stream of defense contracts, reached an all-time high. Gerald's company was making fighter planes for several clients abroad. In the 1990s, however, cutbacks in military spending have rocked the aviation industry. Gerald has seen co-workers suffer pay cuts and, in some cases, get laid off. In addition, doubts have been raised about the security of Gerald's pension plan.

American aviation companies, especially those that depended heavily on military contracts, are eager to find new export markets. Much of their attention has focused on China, where air travel and the demand for aircraft are booming. In addition, American aviation firms hope to revitalize the military sector by strengthening their ties overseas. One project involves a cooperative effort between American and Japanese companies to build a fighter plane, the F-2, for Japan. While the American aviation industry is grateful for Japan's decision to order 130 of the fighters, critics have warned that the United States is relinquishing valuable technology to the Japanese that could harm our country's global competitiveness. Citing the television and VCR industries, they fear that the Japanese will apply what they have learned from the F-2 project to challenge American dominance in military and commercial aircraft sales.

As a resident of Southern California, Gerald is in a unique position to assess the impact of increased foreign trade. He is familiar with the optimistic outlook of many local business leaders. They foresee strong economic growth for the area as the U.S. economy tilts toward the Pacific. The passage of NAFTA has generated greater economic activity along the U.S.-Mexican border, accelerating a trend that began in the mid-1980s. From 1988 to 1991, for example, trade between Mexico and California increased 60 percent to more than $10 billion a year.

Along with growth, however, have come problems. Local companies have moved abroad to avoid U.S. standards on environmental protection and worker safety. Not far from Teresa's hometown in northern Mexico there is an industrial park that houses several factories. Teresa's relatives complain that chemical fumes from the plants pollute the air and that untreated waste water flows into the Pacific Ocean.

Indeed, the industrial belt in northern Mexico near the U.S. border is home to some of the worst pollution in North America. Some corporations have taken advantage of Mexico's comparatively weak environmental laws to avoid the costs involved in addressing industrial pollution. They also know that the agencies assigned to enforce Mexico's environmental laws are seriously understaffed and financially strained. As a result, health experts in Mexico report that factory workers often suffer from ailments related to pollution. American environmentalists maintain that both the pollution and health problems will increasingly extend across the border with the expansion of U.S.-Mexican trade.

The impact of the globalization of the economy is expected to reach into other aspects of American society. For all of our country's problems, the United States offers its citizens much better education and health care than most countries in East Asia and Latin America provide. Economists, however, predict that over time free trade will smooth out some of the differences in the societies of the Pacific Rim.

While free trade supporters expect the WTO, NAFTA, and other trade agreements to gradually raise the standards of poorer countries to those of the United States, Japan, and Canada, critics fear that affluent societies will become more like the developing world.

SECTION 4

Views on U.S. options

Now that you have read about some of the issues related to U.S. trade policy, it is time to take a closer look at what our country's position should be. In this section, you will explore three views on U.S. trade policy. As you will see, each of the views is based on a distinct set of values and beliefs, and is shaped by a well-defined perspective on the threats and opportunities facing the United States.

The views presented address three fundamental questions that frame the discussion on U.S. trade policy:

•**What should be the leading priorities guiding U.S. trade policy?** Should the United States subordinate its trade interests to larger security concerns, as we did during the Cold War, in an effort to promote the health of the international system? Or should U.S. policy concentrate on protecting American industries from global competition, as was generally the case before World War II?

•**What should be the role of the government in the U.S. economy?** Should the government actively favor companies in emerging export-oriented industries? Or should the government maintain a hands-off approach as defenders of free-market competition have advocated?

•**What image of the United States should U.S. trade policy project to the rest of the world?** Should the United States assume the stance of a confident world leader and continue to press for lower trade barriers through the WTO? Or should our country take a more defensive stance toward global competition and seek to guard American interests through protectionist measures or regional trade pacts such as NAFTA?

Each of the three views that follows responds differently to these questions. You should think of the views as a tool designed to help you examine the contrasting strategies from which Americans must define our country's role in the world and craft future policy.

View 1 — Promote free trade

U.S. trade policy should be based on the premise that the United States, as well as the world as a whole, benefits from free trade. Open trade has provided American consumers with better products at lower prices. During the Cold War, the growth of trade cemented alliances among the countries of

Western Europe, East Asia, and the United States. In today's interconnected global economy, free trade is serving to build new bridges between peoples, and, more than ever, the United States is in a position to reap the benefits. Our technological expertise has given us the lead in many promising industries of the future, including biotechnology, telecommunications, and computer software. To back away now from our commitment to free trade would be a setback not only for the United States, but for the entire world.

Considering trade-offs

• Will the laws of the marketplace result in the continued transfer of millions of American manufacturing jobs overseas and further depress the living standards of American workers?

• Will our country be forced to weaken environmental standards and cut education and social services to meet economic competition from poor, developing countries?

• Will blindly pursuing the principles of free trade leave American high-tech industries at a disadvantage in competing against government-supported companies in East Asia and Western Europe?

View 2 — Protect American workers

U.S. trade policy should put the interests of American workers first and fight unfair foreign competition. We can no longer afford to open our doors to imported goods while other countries shield their industries behind high tariffs and impenetrable regulations. The United States has lost its lead in electronics, textiles, steel, and other vital industries. Our country has recorded big trade deficits for well over a decade. The time has come to fight back. U.S. trade policy must put the interests of American workers above the naive goal of free trade. We must focus on stemming the flow of manufacturing jobs overseas and protecting our industries from unfair foreign competition.

Considering trade-offs

• Will protectionist measures in the United States plunge the global economy into a depression by setting off a trade war and reducing the volume of exports worldwide?

• Will erecting barriers against foreign competition send the U.S. economy sliding toward inefficiency and backwardness, as was the case in the Soviet Union?

• Will taking a tough stance toward our trading partners undermine our most important alliances and contribute to international tensions?

View 3 — Chart our economic course

U.S. trade policy should be part of an overall government strategy designed to give our country an edge in high-tech industries. In the world of economics, victory goes to those who adapt to change. As a country, we have to redefine our conception of national security and recognize that our economic future lies at the core of U.S. interests. Changes in the global economy demand a new relationship among government, industry, and universities. Just as governments in East Asia and Western Europe work as partners with business, so too should U.S. leaders from the public and private sectors work together to achieve national economic goals. To develop the technologies of tomorrow, the government must take an active role in identifying areas of promise, investing in research, and promoting exports.

Considering trade-offs

• Will giving government officials the power to pick economic winners and losers favor big corporations with influence in Washington and leave small, innovative companies at a disadvantage?

• Will expanding the government's role in the economy increase the likelihood of multi-billion dollar boondoggles, exacerbate bureaucratic red tape, and open the door to corruption?

• Will focusing on high-tech industries, rather than the needs of workers, add to the budget deficit while doing little to improve the lives of the majority of Americans?

Your turn

These views are by no means the only U.S. options. Rather, they are intended to lay out some of the most important values and assumptions underlying the debate on U.S. trade policy and to spur discussion on the direction our country should take regarding this pressing issue. When you meet next time, you will have an opportunity to discuss U.S. trade policy with others. The following statements are designed to help you clarify your thoughts on what is most important to you concerning this issue. Take a few moments to respond. This is a tool for you to get started. It will not be collected.

Rate each of the statements according to your beliefs:

1 = Strongly Support   3 = Oppose   5 = Undecided

2 = Support   4 = Strongly Oppose

___ More than any other single factor, our country's ability to compete in the global economy will determine the fate of the United States in the coming century.

___ The United States should not trade with nations that grossly abuse the human rights of their citizens.

___ The interests of the United States can be maintained only if we resolutely exercise our power and influence in international affairs.

___ The United States should be willing to give up some of its own sovereignty to promote international cooperation.

___ The economic prosperity of our trading partners contributes to the prosperity of Americans as well.

___ In our competitive economic world, one country's gain is usually another country's loss.

___ The success and failure of trade policy should be judged by how it affects American workers.

___ In our increasingly global economy, we are putting American companies at a disadvantage if we do not provide government support for promising new technologies.

___ The United States cannot afford to give other nations a say in policies by which Americans must live.

Suggested reading

Fallows, James M. *Looking at the Sun: The Rise of the New East Asian Economic and Political System* (New York: Pantheon Books, 1994).

Greider, William. *One World, Ready or Not: The Manic Logic of Global Capitalism* (New York: Simon and Schuster, 1996).

Krueger, Anne O. *American Trade Policy: A Tragedy in the Making* (Washington, D.C.: American Enterprise Institute Press, 1995).

Krugman, Paul R. *Peddling Prosperity: Economic Sense and Nonsense in an Age of Diminished Expectations* (New York: W.W. Norton, 1994).

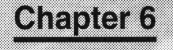

Chapter 6

China on the World Stage: Weighing the U.S. Response

In the late 1970s, China was beginning to emerge from three decades of economic isolation imposed by Mao Ze-dong. Mao's policies had produced a society in which equality and uniformity were highly valued. China was able to feed and clothe its population, the largest in the world, but there were few opportunities for individual advancement.

At the time of Mao's death in 1976, Li Xiao-hua was a peasant working on a state-run wheat farm in northern China. Like millions of his countrymen, Li closely followed the struggle for power among China's political elite that followed Mao's death. He was pleased when Deng Xiao-ping emerged at the head of China's Communist Party, and he supported Deng's program of economic reform.

Today, Li is a symbol of China's transformation since the late 1970s. Li drives around Beijing, China's capital, in a red Ferrari. He has become a

A Meeting of Opposites

Historically, the Chinese have called their country the Middle Kingdom and have considered themselves at the center of civilization. Until the 1800s, their view was largely justified. Chinese culture was unmatched in its continuity and refinement. The Chinese system of government was remarkable for its ability to maintain order, manage an efficient bureaucracy, and build roads, bridges, and canals over a vast empire.

At the time Columbus was exploring the Americas, China seemed poised to move on to still greater accomplishments. The Chinese were responsible for many of the most important inventions of the modern age — the compass, printing, and gunpowder among them. Chinese ships in the late 15th century were superior to those being produced in Europe, and Chinese sea captains were expanding China's trade ties throughout Asia. Moreover, China's unified empire stood in sharp contrast to the feuding kingdoms of Europe.

Yet as Europe turned outward to conquer new territories and probe the frontiers of science, China turned inward. China remained a country of rich traditions and great wealth, but the Chinese cut themselves off from the extraordinary advances occurring in Western Europe. Just how far China had fallen behind the West was not evident until the so-called Opium Wars of the 19th century.

A century of humiliation

The Opium War of 1839-42, triggered by China's attempt to stop the British opium trade, shattered the illusion of Chinese superiority. British warships leveled Chinese coastal defenses and destroyed the Chinese southern fleet. The result was the first in a series of one-sided treaties between China and the West. At the time, China's defeat in the Opium War was viewed by many in the Manchu dynasty as an accident. They failed to understand that their empire had been strained to the breaking point by rapid population growth and frequent rebellions. Instead, they stumbled into the second

multi-millionaire real-estate developer and monitors his business empire with computers, fax machines, and cellular phones.

Mao would be stunned. The China he left behind strictly forbade private enterprise. Private cars were unheard of. As late as 1981, only twenty people in Beijing owned their own vehicles. The China that Deng and Li have helped to create now has 3 million private vehicles, with another 8 million cars, vans, and trucks belonging to either business enterprises or the government. Annual vehicle sales now approach 1.5 million.

The vast majority of China's 1.2 billion people remain poor by American standards, but the pace of economic reform has turned China into an economic giant. China's economy is comparable in size to that of Japan, placing it second or third in the world. In the last fifteen years, China's economic growth has averaged 9 percent annually. No major country in modern times has grown so fast for such a long period. If present trends continue, China

Opium War in 1857. Although the Chinese put up a more concerted defense, Western forces fought their way to Beijing, burned and looted the Summer Palace, and forced the emperor to flee.

China's weakness was undeniable. By the late 19th century, China was helpless to fend off the ambitions of the imperial powers of Europe, Japan, and the United States. China's defeat at the hands of Japan in 1894 was especially demoralizing. Japan's military success, along with spiraling competition among European nations, stirred anxiety among U.S. officials that Americans would be shut out of the Chinese market. In 1899, Secretary of State John Hay sent a note to the foreign powers in China requesting that they maintain an "open door" in their spheres of influence. The Open Door note served as the foundation of U.S. policy toward China for the next half century.

The United States was a source of both inspiration and resentment for the new generation of intellectuals that set the tone of the Chinese nationalist movement in the early 1900s. The

American ideals of democracy and equal opportunity were admired by Chinese intellectuals, yet they recognized that many American officials viewed them with disdain.

The nationalists toppled the Manchu dynasty in 1911. However, they lacked the strength to carry out their plans to form a stable constitutional republic. Instead, China was to be riven by civil war for much of the next four decades.

The Kuomintang (or Nationalist Party) and Chinese Communist Party eventually came to dominate Chinese politics. In the mid-1920s, Chiang Kai-shek, the Kuomintang leader, assembled the military might to subdue China's regional warlords and clamp down on the communists. By 1928, Chiang was strong enough to declare himself the ruler of China.

China's unity, however, was soon to face a renewed threat from Japan. In 1931, the Japanese imposed their control over Manchuria. Six years later, they plunged deeper into China's heartland, quickly forcing Chiang to abandon his capital of Nanjing. America's growing ties to

will overtake the United States as the world's leading economic producer by 2020.

China's transformation is changing international relations almost as fast as it is changing the lives of the Chinese people. For much of human history, China has been the richest, most powerful country in the world. During the 19th and early 20th centuries, however, China suffered from foreign domination after falling behind the rapidly industrializing countries of Europe, the United States, and Japan. Today, China is again reasserting its influence in world affairs. Just as the 1900s have been referred to as the "American century," the year 2001 may mark the beginning of the "Chinese century."

The implications for the United States are enormous. Americans have already felt the impact of China's economic boom. China was our country's fourth-largest trading partner in 1996 (following Canada, Japan, and Mexico). Chinese-made clothing, shoes, and toys fill American stores, while China has become an important customer for our country's aircraft and telecommunications industries. At the same time, disputes over China's failure to accept international trade standards and Beijing's poor human rights record have frequently threatened to boil over into a trade war.

China, forged largely by investors and Protestant missionaries, evoked public outrage at Japan's aggression. Nonetheless, the administration of Franklin D. Roosevelt was careful to avoid conflict with Tokyo in the 1930s.

Japan's attack on Pearl Harbor in 1941 finally brought the United States into the war on the side of China. Over the next four years, American military advisers and equipment strengthened the resistance of the Chinese army. The China front, however, remained an area of low priority for U.S. military planners. The large-scale commitment of American troops that Chiang lobbied for never arrived. Indeed, the Japanese army at the end of World War II was still firmly entrenched in China.

The United States made sure that Chiang's government was given a prominent place in the postwar international system, pressing for China's inclusion in the Security Council at the founding meeting of the United Nations. Washington, though, was unable to prevent the long-simmering civil war between the Kuomintang and the communists from erupting in 1946. As most American officials had predicted, Mao Ze-dong's communist forces soon gained the upper hand. By 1949, Chiang's army was in a panicked retreat, leaving behind most of its U.S.-supplied equipment.

Communist China

As the communists overran southern China in 1949, the administration of Harry Truman decided that further aid to Chiang was useless. Truman expected that the communists would soon gain control over Formosa (present-day Taiwan) as well. After Mao proclaimed the People's Republic of China in October 1949, U.S. leaders concentrated on driving a wedge between Mao and the Soviet Union.

Of perhaps greater significance for the future is China's place on the world stage. Under communist rule, China has built up the world's largest army in terms of manpower while holding down spending on high-tech equipment. China's defense budget still amounts to roughly one-tenth of the U.S. level, but in recent years purchases of new weapons have risen sharply. Moreover, China has pressed ahead with plans to modernize its nuclear arsenal. U.S. officials fear that the coming generation of Chinese leaders may seek to flex China's military muscle in East Asia and beyond.

The outlook for U.S.-Chinese relations is also complicated by China's leadership transition. The death of Deng Xiao-ping in 1997 has opened a vacuum in Chinese politics. China's president, Jiang Ze-min, seems unlikely to command the authority of Deng. Instead, competing factions within the Communist Party, the military, and regional governments are expected to vie for power. Without a paramount leader in Beijing, the policies of economic reform and rapprochement with the United States fashioned by Deng may be jeopardized.

China's economic future is uncertain too. Rapid growth has overheated the economy, triggering bursts of inflation. Sharp divisions have opened up

Communist North Korea's invasion of South Korea in June 1950 changed U.S. policy in East Asia overnight. The U.S. entry into the war was followed in September 1950 by Chinese involvement. Before a truce was reached in 1953, roughly 250,000 Chinese and 54,000 American troops had died in the fighting. Bitter enmity was to set the tone of U.S.-Chinese relations for the next two decades. The United States signed defense treaties with most of China's neighbors and stationed tens of thousands of troops in South Korea, Japan, and Taiwan. In 1954 and 1958, the United States pledged to use force to counter Chinese threats to invade two small islands claimed by Taiwan. U.S. leaders explained America's growing involvement in the Vietnam War largely in terms of the threat posed by China.

Ironically, the initiative to change the U.S. stance toward China came from President Richard Nixon. Nixon was eager to realign the global balance of power at a time when Soviet influence was on the rise. Nixon's visit to Beijing in 1972 followed two years of exploratory talks. Deng Xiao-ping's claim on leadership after Mao's death in 1976 signalled that further progress was possible.

Deng quietly assured U.S. officials that China would not use force against Taiwan. The United States responded in 1979 by officially recognizing China — and by withdrawing recognition from Taiwan. The future of Taiwan remained a sticking point in U.S.-Chinese relations during much of the 1980s. At the same time, expanding trade and investment, as well as a surge in student, scientific, and cultural exchanges, were fast creating important links between the two countries. China was not a U.S. ally, but a new era in U.S.-Chinese relations was clearly underway. ❑

in society, pitting the rich against the poor, city dwellers against farmers, and the prosperous southeastern coast against the struggling interior. The central government is burdened by huge state-run enterprises that employ tens of millions of workers, while its control over the private sector of the economy continues to slip. The transfer of Hong Kong to Beijing's control in 1997 is certain to highlight the contradictions of China's economic system. Even many successful Chinese businessmen worry that the underpinnings of the current economic boom will give way beneath them.

Consideration of our country's policy toward China requires attention to both the immediate challenges before us and the direction of U.S.-Chinese relations over the long term. For the moment, trade disputes, the transfer of Hong Kong, human rights abuses, China's position in East Asia, and the control of nuclear arms are featured in the daily headlines. But what about U.S.-Chinese relations in the next century? How should Americans view China — as a valued trading partner, as a rival superpower, as a source of instability and conflict? Since the end of the Cold War, this question has moved toward the top of the U.S. foreign policy agenda.

China's transformation

China's history in the 20th century is woven into the life of Deng Xiaoping. Deng was an early member of the Chinese Communist Party and fought both Chiang Kai-shek's forces and the Japanese army during the 1930s and 1940s. In 1968, at the height of China's Cultural Revolution, he was forced to confess to being a "counter-revolutionary" and was driven out of Beijing. For six years, Deng was denied the position he had held in the Politburo, the ruling body of the Communist Party. He returned to the leadership ranks only to come under attack in 1976 as "the unrepentant capitalist-roader." For the next two years, Deng and his political opponents grappled for power as the fate of China hung in the balance.

And yet, at the end of 1978, already 74 years old and still securing his leadership, Deng took on the biggest struggle of his career: reforming the Chinese economy. Deng had long been known as a pragmatist within the Communist Party. He was especially critical of the radicals who stressed the need to purify communist ideology. Instead, he was a champion of policies that would advance China's development.

Economic reform

Deng gradually dismantled Mao's command economy. The impact of his reforms was felt first in the countryside, home to 70 percent of China's people. Instead of large collective farms, individual families were given responsibility for working the land through long-term leases. Price controls were lifted and peasants were allowed to sell most of their crop in the marketplace. The "work units" that controlled housing, health care, education, and other necessities of life in the countryside were abolished. In addition, people in the countryside were allowed to open their own businesses outside of agriculture. Progress came quickly. Within seven years, output in rural areas had shot up by 48 percent.

Success in agriculture encouraged Deng to extend his reforms to industry and commerce. Deng opened China up to the global economy. Special economic zones were created along the southeastern coast that allowed Chinese entrepreneurs and foreign investors to go into business with little government interference. Exports were promoted. Central economic planners lost much of their authority to officials at the local and provincial levels. Across China, millions of new enterprises were established. Many were offshoots of state-run factories, universities, collective farms, or other institutions of the communist system.

By Ma Long. Reprinted from *Seeds of Fire.*

Deng's reforms went a long way toward bringing China into the global marketplace. Exports rose from $14 billion in 1979 to $151 billion in 1996. China ranked 11th worldwide in manufactured exports in 1996, with 3 percent of the global market. (If exports from Hong Kong had been included, China would have ranked fourth.)

Deng Xiao-ping returned to prominence from political oblivion in 1978.

China has also led developing countries in attracting foreign investment, garnering $38 billion in 1995.

American investors have played a leading role in China's economic boom, but in recent years investments from Hong Kong and Taiwan have grown at an even faster pace. Most Hong Kong manufacturers, for example, now make their products inside China in neighboring Guangdong province.

Between communism and capitalism

Deng labeled his country's economic system "socialism with Chinese characteristics." In fact, neither economic analysts nor government regulators have been able to keep up with China's economic transformation. In many respects, China today is moving swiftly toward the free-market economic system. Most decisions about what goods are going to be produced and how much they will cost are made by producers and consumers, not by government planners.

In other ways, features of the communist system continue to define China. Most city workers, for example, obtain their housing through their workplaces and pay very little rent. The government provides free health care in most cases and steps in to prevent sharp increases in food prices.

Most important, about one-third of China's industrial output is produced by state-owned factories. Many of them are outdated and inefficient giants with tens of thousands of workers. The Anshan Iron and Steel Mills in northeastern China alone employs 500,000 people. Half of the companies in the state sector are losing money. Under Mao, workers in the big state-owned factories were celebrated for propelling China toward industrialization. They were poor, but they were guaranteed the benefits of what was known as the "iron rice bowl" — a secure job, free housing, and health care.

The government has prodded managers in the state sector to respond more effectively to free-market forces, but has backed away from carrying out the deep job cutbacks that economists recommend. There are roughly 90 million Chinese without work, and officials fear that increasing unemployment could lead to widespread unrest.

Unemployment would be much worse in China if not for the startling growth of the non-state sector of the economy. Most non-state enterprises fall

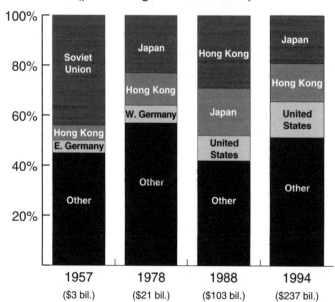

China's Leading Trading Partners
(percentage of total trade)

Data from *China in the Era of Deng Xiaoping* and the Department of Commerce

into two categories. The privately owned sector most closely resembles businesses in our own country. It consists of enterprises under the ownership of Chinese entrepreneurs, foreign investors, or Chinese-foreign joint ventures. Most of these firms are located in southeastern China.

More difficult to grasp is the economic sector that belongs neither to the state nor to private entrepreneurs. Many villages and towns in the countryside, for example, have branched out into other businesses. Although in theory they are public enterprises, they are not managed or funded by the government. In the cities, workers at state institutions are finding similar opportunities.

For example, professors from the engineering department of a univer-

Courtesy of Anita Malkasian

A member of China's newly prosperous merchant class.

sity may decide to open a small factory producing machine parts. If their business prospers, they will likely take home profits that are many times above their university salaries. The question of ownership, however, usually remains unclear. Is the factory a private or a state enterprise? And who decides how the profits — or the potential losses — are shared?

Society in a whirlwind

Even with much of China's economy on unsteady ground, the impact of economic growth is clearly evident, especially in the cities. A generation ago, Chinese consumers aspired to own a bicycle, a wristwatch, and a radio. Today, Chinese set their sights on color televisions, refrigerators, and VCRs.

Chinese in all walks of life, from teachers to doctors to tractor drivers, have decided to go into business, or as the Chinese say, "plunge into the sea." Chinese society has turned its back on many of the guiding principles of communism, and introduced a new emphasis on materialism and individualism.

Corruption among government officials is now widespread. The combination of dedication, discipline, and fear that served to restrain China's bureaucrats under Mao has largely broken down. Many of them resent the sudden wealth of the country's new entrepreneurs and have sought a piece of the action for themselves by demanding bribes for export licenses, building permits, and other government documents. Hundreds of thousands more have taken advantage of their authority to set up their own businesses. A few have embezzled millions of dollars in state funds and fled overseas.

Meanwhile, Chinese officials are losing the battle to control the thinking of their citizens. The opening of China's economy has exposed the country to the forces of the information revolution. Fax machines, television satellite dishes, computer modems, and short-wave radios have linked China to the outside world. Chinese-language news and entertainment from Hong Kong pour over the airwaves into China. Most observers believe that Beijing's decisions to ban the ownership of satellite dishes and censor the reports of foreign news services has come too late to stop the flood. In addition, the influx of foreign business executives, tourists, and students has introduced millions of Chinese to life abroad.

Collapse of communist values

China's new openness has left the greatest impression on the young. The generation of Chinese youth that has grown up in the last fifteen years has faced a bewildering shift in values. Whereas communist slogans and portraits of Mao once held sway over city streets, customers in private shops today are more likely to encounter posters of Hollywood movie stars and *Playboy* pin-ups.

Many Chinese youth, especially in the cities, voice their feelings by embracing what is known as "grey culture" — a defiant contrast to the official culture sponsored by the Communist Party. Grey culture is expressed mostly through punkish fashions, pop art, offbeat fiction, and rock 'n' roll.

The evolution of grey culture has reflected the course of Chinese political life. In 1987, the government launched the "anti-bourgeois liberalization campaign" to rid China of "spiritual pollution" from abroad. The tide of the information revolution soon forced the authorities to retreat on the cultural front, but they continued to hold the line against political reform.

In the spring of 1989, they were challenged by a loosely organized democracy movement led by university students. By early June, the movement had taken the form of a mass demonstration in Tiananmen Square in the center of Beijing. Cui Jian, China's most well-known rock performer, played before the crowd wearing a red blindfold. Students erected a replica of the Statue of Liberty to symbolize their quest for democracy. The government responded by calling in the army to break up the protest. Troops killed dozens of people in the square and hundreds of others in nearby streets. Thousands more were arrested.

New divisions

China's generation gap is only one of many divisions that have opened up in society since the late 1970s. More serious is the widening gulf between rich and poor. Chinese cities are home today to stark contrasts, just as they were before the communist revolution. Homeless beggars can be found outside the storefronts of millionaire businessmen. Expensive nightclubs have opened up for the new elite while ordinary Chinese complain about the dramatic rise in violent crime, drug use, and prostitution.

In the countryside, Chinese peasants look to the cities with envy. Although farmers were the first to benefit from Deng's economic reforms,

Bettmann

A Beijing citizen stares down a column of tanks approaching Tiananmen Square.

progress in agriculture has slowed since the mid-1980s. In many areas, the breakup of collective farms has held back the modernization of agriculture because investment in roads, irrigation canals, and grain silos has declined. In addition, crop prices have not kept up with the cost of manufactured goods. The average Chinese peasant earns only about one-tenth of the income of city dwellers along China's southeastern coast. Many Chinese villagers hang portraits of Mao in their homes to symbolize their discontent.

Since Deng's government gradually freed peasants from travel restrictions, millions of villagers have joined a new class of rootless migrants who are either without land of their own or looking for opportunity. There are as many as 150 million of them now looking for work, often floating from city to city. Downtown streets in major Chinese cities are full of "one-day mules" — young men available for day labor at low wages.

In southeastern China, the destination of most migrants from the countryside, conditions recall scenes from the sweatshops of New York or the slaughterhouses of Chicago in the late 1800s. Young women looking for a factory job can expect to work long hours on an assembly line and to sleep in a crowded dormitory above the factory floor. Wages are as low as $1 a day. Moreover, party officials often collect under-the-table fees of $1,000 to arrange employment. Many of the young men and women who do not find a niche in the economy are sucked into China's growing underclass of criminals, drug addicts, and prostitutes.

Political uncertainty

China's economic transformation has brought the country to a political crossroads. The values of Mao Ze-dong no longer hold China together. The generation of influential elders that led the communist revolution is dying out. The vision of a strong, self-reliant communist society has been largely abandoned by the generation that has grown up under Deng Xiao-ping. For the time being, the Communist Party remains in control, but its ideology has faded and its authority at the regional and local levels has waned. Meanwhile, there is no clear political roadmap to guide China into the future.

If the experience of China's East Asian neighbors holds true, pressure for democracy will gradually build as economic progress draws more Chinese into the middle class. South Korea and Taiwan, for example, emerged as economic powerhouses under the rule of one-party dictatorships, but now appear headed toward democratic reform.

In the short term, democracy is seen as less of a threat to the authority

Reprinted from *Seeds of Fire*

Prisoner #1: "What are you here for?"
Prisoner #2: "I opposed Hu Yao-bang. And you?"
Prisoner #3: "I supported him. (Addressing Prisoner #1) What about you?"
Prisoner #1: "I am Hu Yao-bang."

(Hu Yao-bang was forced to resign as head of the Chinese Communist Party in 1987 after pushing to speed up the pace of reform.)

of the Chinese Communist Party than is the increasing concentration of power at the provincial and local levels. China's wealthy southeastern provinces, such as Guangdong, hold onto almost all of their tax revenues and receive little from the central government in return. In a few cases, regional trade wars have erupted, with provincial governments imposing tariffs on goods from neighboring provinces. Smuggling has frustrated Beijing's efforts to collect taxes. In 1994, for example, Chinese officials estimate that 80 billion foreign cigarettes were imported illegally into their country.

Meanwhile, China's national budget deficits have ballooned in recent years. Many of the big state-run factories that supply much of the revenue for the central government are themselves failing. China's leaders are even more worried that the central command of the Chinese army may dissolve, giving rise to the emergence of regional warlords.

The uncertainty at the top adds to the mood of anxiety. Deng left to his successors many of the most difficult items on the economic reform agenda. The circle around President Jiang Ze-min, however, lacks both the political will and the prestige to follow through on critical measures, such as imposing the rule of law, limiting the power of the Communist Party, and trimming the state sector of the economy.

The Beijing leadership must also keep the peace with rival centers of power. Conservatives within the military, the party bureaucracy, and state-run industries favor slowing the pace of change and reasserting the authority of the party. They face opposition from regional leaders and business tycoons who are riding the wave of China's boom.

SECTION 2

The U.S.-Chinese agenda

With 22 percent of the world's population, the second- or third-largest economy, and a nuclear arsenal undergoing modernization, China is destined to enter the 21st century as a leading focus for policymakers in the United States and elsewhere.

What remains to be seen, however, is what kind of China will take shape from the present tumult. A strong, confident China could act as a force for peace and stability in East Asia and serve as an expanding market for high-tech American exports. Or it could become a regional bully and increasingly seek to challenge U.S. interests around the world. Conversely, a weak, unstable China presents another set of threats. An economic crisis in China could send shock waves throughout the global economy, especially in East Asia. Tens of millions of economic refugees could spill beyond China's borders, with millions of them heading for the United States. A collapse of political authority could draw the world's great powers into the confusion, just as it did in the 19th century.

Americans are confronted with a particularly difficult task in charting our country's policy toward China. First, we must keep a close watch on developments inside of China during this time of change. Second, we must consider our own country's role in the world and our relationship with a China that is poised to acquire the strength of a global superpower some time in the next century.

Trade tensions

For the next few years at least, trade issues are expected to dominate the U.S.-Chinese agenda. Many of them are very recent in their origins. During Mao's rule, trade between the two countries was meager. Throughout the 1980s, it grew steadily, with a fairly even balance between imports and exports.

Recent years, however, have witnessed a surge in Chinese exports.

Americans in 1996 bought $51.5 billion in Chinese products — over one-third of China's exports worldwide. Most of the Chinese-made goods were low-priced manufactured items, such as clothing, toys, bicycles, shoes, consumer electronics, and kitchenware. China's labor costs in manufacturing average less than 50 cents an hour, compared to more than $18 an hour in the United States. The U.S. trade deficit with China widened to $39.5 billion in 1996 — second only to our country's trade deficit with Japan.

American exports to China have expanded rapidly as well, approaching $12 billion in 1996. Boeing, McDonnell Douglas, and other aviation companies have recorded billions of dollars in aircraft sales to the Chinese in the 1990s. Communications giant AT&T views China — not the United States — as its fastest-growing market.

Even as U.S.-Chinese trade ties multiply, the attitudes of the two countries toward international commerce remain sharply divided. While U.S. leaders have strongly defended the principle of free trade, China has imposed import tariffs averaging 40 percent. In recent years, Chinese leaders have taken steps to bring their country into the global economic mainstream.

China has applied to join the World Trade Organization (WTO), the body that sets the ground rules for global trade and includes more than 130 member states. The Beijing government hopes to be admitted as a poor, developing country, meaning that China would be given extra time to lower protectionist trade barriers. In 1995, Beijing announced that its import tariffs would be cut by approximately 30 percent on more than 4,000 items.

Chinese leaders have looked to the United States to back their country's admission into the WTO for the sake of stable international relations. However, President Clinton and other world leaders are opposed to concessions for Beijing. They maintain that China's export muscle proves that the Chinese are ready to play by the same

U.S. Trade with China

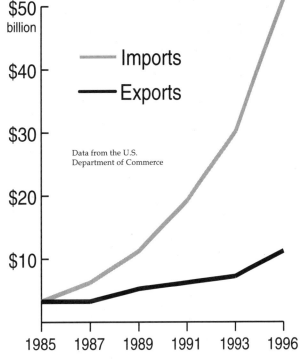

Data from the U.S.
Department of Commerce

rules accepted by wealthy, developed countries.

U.S. pressure on China has brought the two countries to the brink of a trade war in recent years over violations of intellectual property rights in China. American music industry executives charge that 220 million cassette tapes and 45 million compact discs were copied illegally in China in 1995. U.S. computer software producers estimate that Chinese pirate operations turned out $525 million in American-designed computer programs in 1995. Prompted by U.S. threats to raise tariffs on more than $1 billion worth of Chinese exports, Beijing has carried out several well-publicized raids on copyright pirates. American business groups, however, contend that the crackdowns are largely for show. They claim that companies profiting from copyright pirating are often closely connected to the military, secret police, and local governments.

In addition to concern about intellectual property rights violations, U.S. officials have complained that Chinese clothing manufacturers frequently sell their goods below cost on the international market to force out competition. China also contributes to the destruction of endangered wildlife by importing rhinoceros horns, tiger organs, and other animal parts for use in Chinese folk medicines.

Human rights issues

China's human rights record has been a central feature of the U.S.-Chinese trade picture since 1989. After the government crackdown against protesters in Tiananmen Square, President George Bush stopped sales of U.S. military equipment to China. Anger in Congress toward the Chinese leadership was much stronger. Many Congressional representatives favored linking China's human rights performance to U.S.-Chinese trade relations. They threatened to end China's most-favored-nation status as a means of pressuring China's leaders to change their policies at home.

Human rights organizations have drawn up a long list of complaints against China. Their sources indicate that China holds thousands of political prisoners, many of whom were active in the democracy movement of 1989. China also has a history of using prison labor to manufacture export goods.

Of particular concern is China's policy toward the region of Tibet. The Tibetans enjoyed autonomy for centuries, but in 1950 Chinese troops over-ran their homeland. Communist officials have attempted to erase Tibet's distinctive culture. After a rebellion in 1959, hundreds of thousands of Tibetans were killed or imprisoned. Thousands of monasteries, temples, and other examples of Tibetan architecture also were destroyed. Since the 1980s, Beijing's policies have been aimed at promoting the migration of thousands of ethnic Chinese to Tibet. The Tibetans are now a minority in the region.

As a candidate for the presidency in 1992, Bill Clinton argued that China's most-favored-nation status should be linked to Beijing's human rights record. As president, he signed an executive order in 1993 that required China to achieve "significant progress" on human rights in order for its most-favored-nation status to be renewed in 1994. The top U.S. priorities were China's use of prison labor and the emigration restrictions that prevented leading Chinese political dissidents from leaving the country. The United States also raised the issues of Tibet, the treatment of political prisoners, and the jamming of radio and television broadcasts from abroad.

However, when the showdown came over China's trade status in May 1994, President Clinton retreated. He conceded that China had not met the conditions called for in his executive order, but he went ahead and renewed China's most-favored-nation status. He also announced that he would reject efforts to link U.S.-Chinese trade with human rights issues in the future.

Most American business leaders praised Clinton's decision. They contend that American companies cannot afford to be shut out of the Chinese market, especially when there is little support internationally for a tough stance on human rights. In contrast, human rights organizations make the case that the United States is giving up an opportunity to steer China toward greater openness and freedom.

China's Exports to the U.S.

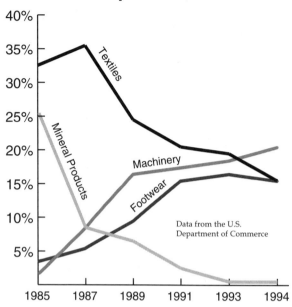

Data from the U.S. Department of Commerce

Security issues

While trade and human rights issues have dominated the headlines of U.S.-Chinese relations, U.S. policymakers have often placed more emphasis on military concerns. China's defense budget has increased steadily in the 1990s, growing at about the same rate as the overall economy. In 1996, Beijing spent from $20 to $25 billion on its military.

By all accounts, China is many years away from matching the technological sophistication of the U.S. military. Its defense spending, according to most estimates, is still behind that of Japan. Chinese leaders, however, seem committed to a long-term program of military modernization. Their policies could soon tip the balance of power in East Asia.

China's nuclear weapons have attracted particular attention. In terms of explosive force, China has the third most powerful nuclear arsenal in the world. (China has 450 nuclear warheads, compared to 10,400 for Russia and 9,150 for the United States.)

Although the other major nuclear powers stopped testing their weapons in 1992, Chinese leaders plan to conduct additional tests as part of their efforts to develop a nuclear missile with multiple warheads and a longer range submarine-launched missile. Indian leaders fear that China's growing nuclear might is directed against their own country and, in turn, have pressed ahead with India's nuclear program.

China has also become a key player in the international arms market. Since the collapse of the Soviet Union, China has become a major customer for high-tech Russian military equipment. Beijing has been especially eager to acquire Russian nuclear missile technology.

At the same time, Chinese weapons exports are well-known worldwide. According to the Central Intelligence Agency (CIA), China is the largest source of technology for developing countries seeking to build up arsenals of long-range missiles, chemical weapons, or nuclear bombs. CIA evidence also indicates that China has played a key role in helping Pakistan produce missiles capable of delivering nuclear warheads within a range of 185 miles.

The Clinton administration has avoided a direct confrontation with Beijing over Chinese arms sales. In 1997, Clinton chose to impose sanctions on two Chinese companies, rather than on the Beijing government, for supplying Iran with ingredients for the manufacture of poison gas. U.S. officials warned that stronger action would aggravate the rift between the central government in Beijing and the increasingly independent Chinese military. China's decision to approve the Nuclear Non-Proliferation Treaty was seen as a positive sign that China is willing to cooperate with the United States and its allies in controlling the spread of nuclear weapons.

China's role in the world

Under Mao Ze-dong, China presented itself as a model for the poor, developing countries of the Third World. The image, however, never sat well with many Chinese. They preferred to think of China as a country with a tradition of past greatness that would eventually return to its former status. Chinese leaders in recent years have indeed begun to reassert their country's voice in international relations, primarily in East Asia.

China has been especially bold in staking its claims to two chains of tiny islands in the South China Sea. The islands, known as the Spratlys and the Paracels, reportedly lie atop rich oil deposits. Five of China's neighbors — Vietnam, the Philippines, Taiwan, Malaysia, and Brunei — have made their own claims on the islands, but China has shown little willingness to negotiate a settlement. In 1988, China seized six of the islands in the Spratly chain.

More recently, Beijing has undertaken a build-up of its navy and has increased its presence in the South China Sea. China's attention to its naval forces has U.S. officials worried. A Chinese bid to challenge U.S. dominance could set off an arms race in the region.

Hong Kong and Taiwan also figure prominently on the U.S.-Chinese agenda. In 1997, the British returned Hong Kong to China after controlling the territory for 150 years. Reunification will be complicated. The former colony of nearly 6 million people is an international financial and manufacturing center. Before reunification, it was the largest single foreign investor in China and the gateway for much of China's international trade. Politically, Hong Kong's residents have shown their determination to defend the democratic freedoms they won in the last years of British rule.

China's leaders are eager to take advantage of Hong Kong's economic power and yet are worried about the former colony's dynamism and appeal. The Beijing government has promised to preserve Hong Kong's uniqueness through a policy of "one country, two systems." U.S. officials have voiced concern that China may snuff out Hong Kong's open society. From Beijing's perspective, the fear seems to be that Hong Kong's vibrant brand of capitalism and democracy may fuel momentum for political change in China. Indeed, most of the Chinese troops stationed in the former colony have been positioned to block Chinese from flooding into Hong Kong.

The status of Taiwan represents a more long-term problem in East Asian affairs. Since losing its seat in the United Nations to China in 1971, Taiwan has existed in a sort of international limbo. Economically, it is a powerhouse. The country is one of the top ten exporters in the world and its 21 million people enjoy a per capita income about five times higher than that of the citizens of China.

The governments of Taiwan and China, however, both officially maintain that they represent China. Foreign countries and international organizations have been forced to choose which government to recognize. Since the United States broke relations with Taiwan in 1978, Taipei has found itself largely ostracized in international diplomacy. Taiwan has responded to the shift in policy by seeking to strengthen its economic and cultural ties worldwide. Taiwan's economy has continued to boom, even though Taipei has been forced out of the International Monetary Fund, the World Bank, and other international organizations.

Officially, China, Taiwan, and the United States are committed to the eventual reunification of China and Taiwan. The lack of progress toward reunification, however, has convinced Taiwanese leaders that they should think of their country as an independent state separate from China. In recent years, they have explored the possibility of rejoining the United Nations. Beijing has insisted that reunification must be the ultimate goal, but has welcomed the billions of dollars that Taiwanese businesses have invested in China. Chinese leaders have also lowered barriers to travel and communications between their country and Taiwan.

While military tensions between China and Taiwan have cooled since the 1950s, the potential for conflict remains significant. China's naval expansion has raised concerns in Taipei. For its part, Taiwan has built a defense force of 425,000 troops equipped with sophisticated weapons, many of them from the United States. U.S. arms sales to Taiwan have been a constant irritant in U.S.-Chinese relations.

International position

China's seat on the UN Security Council gives Beijing veto power over critical decisions of the UN. Generally, the Beijing government has gone along with the other members of the Security Council since the end of the Cold War. Before the 1991 Persian Gulf War, for example, the Chinese did not block U.S. efforts to form an international coalition against Iraq's Saddam Hussein. China, however, has yet to contribute troops to a UN peacekeeping mission.

Closer to home for China's leaders has been the confrontation over North Korea's development of nuclear weapons. China joined with the United States and Japan in 1994 to pressure North Korea's communist leadership to freeze its nuclear program in exchange for two nuclear energy reactors. China's exports of oil and food to North Korea give Beijing a crucial role in negotiations with North Korea.

China's economic growth has also become an international issue. China has fueled its industrial expansion mainly with coal. From 1970 to 1990, China's energy consumption rose 208 percent. China now produces more than 12 percent of the world's carbon dioxide emissions, and is expected to surpass the United States as the leading emitter of greenhouse gases within twenty-five years.

China is already shaking up the international market for energy and food. Since the mid-1970s, China's population control program has substantially lowered the country's birth rate. Nonetheless, China's population of 1.2 billion continues to grow by about 12 million annually. Meanwhile, China's new wealth has allowed the Chinese people to become more demanding consumers, turning China into an importer of oil and food. The trend is likely to continue. China is expected to have nearly 50 million vehicles by 2010, pushing it into the ranks of a major oil importer. In addition, China will have to import more grain to feed livestock as prosperous Chinese acquire a greater appetite for meat.

Section 4

Views on U.S. options

Now that you have read about some of the issues related to U.S. policy toward China, it is time to take a closer look at what our country's position should be. In this section, you will explore four views on U.S. policy toward

China. As you will see, each of the views is based on a distinct set of values and beliefs, and is shaped by a well-defined perspective on the threats and opportunities facing the United States.

The views presented address three fundamental questions that frame the discussion on U.S. policy toward China:

•**Should the United States strive to implant American values in China?** Should the United States seek to nudge China toward democracy, respect for human rights, free-market economic reform, tolerance for diversity, and other Western norms? Or should U.S. leaders accept that American values cannot and should not be transplanted to a culture so different from our own?

•**Should our interest in U.S.-Chinese trade drive U.S. policy?** Should U.S. policy focus on cultivating healthy U.S.-Chinese trade relations and expanding American exports to China? Or should trade take a back seat to concerns about China's position in the international arena and dismal human rights record?

•**What should be the tone of U.S. policy toward China?** Should the United States lean hard on Beijing in hopes of steering China in a more suitable direction? Or should the United States approach China with caution, fearful that increased foreign pressure could aggravate the turmoil within China and contribute to an international crisis?

Each of the four views that follows responds differently to these questions. You should think of the views as a tool designed to help you examine the contrasting strategies from which Americans must define our country's role in the world and craft future policy.

View 1 — Press for democratic values

China and the world are at a historic crossroads. As Americans, we must ask ourselves what kind of China we want to see emerge from this period of transition. The choices are stark. The leaders of China's democratic movement are counting on us to take a firm stand against Beijing's communist dictatorship. The people of Tibet are looking to us to help stop the Chinese government's campaign to wipe out their ancient culture. The United States cannot flinch from its commitment to the values we as a nation represent. By applying the leverage we hold, we have an opportunity to promote a new generation of Chinese leaders that recognizes the necessity of creating a more open, democratic society.

Considering trade-offs

•Will using trade policy as a tool to promote human rights spark an anti-American backlash in China and other East Asian countries that do not share our values?

•Will focusing U.S. policy on promoting democratic reform in China distract our leaders from the urgent need to contain China's power and influence?

•Will restricting Chinese exports to the United States lead Beijing to raise its own trade barriers against American products, thus allowing our economic competitors to expand their share of the Chinese market at the expense of U.S. companies?

View 2 — *Promote stability and trade*

China is walking on a tightrope. For the coming decades, the world's most populous country will be teetering above a black hole of chaos and turmoil. In this time of uncertainty, the United States must act as a helpful guide to ensure that China safely reaches a future of stability and prosperity. Our country has a large stake in China's economic health. The importance of our relationship with China demands that the United States proceed with understanding and caution in dealing with Beijing. We must support China's full participation in the institutions of the international community and take measures to strengthen the economic ties between our two countries.

Considering trade-offs

•Will helping the dictatorship in Beijing give Chinese leaders a green light to crush their opponents and encourage tyrants around the world to crack down against supporters of democracy and human rights?

•Will cooperating with China result in the restoration of Beijing's past greatness and come back to haunt us when a Chinese superpower challenges U.S. interests?

•Will ignoring China's violations of international trade standards worsen our country's trade deficit with China, rob American companies of their markets, and cost thousands of American workers their jobs?

View 3 — *Tame the dragon*

China and the United States are on a collision course. With the largest population in the world, expanding military power, and a leadership that is committed to restoring China's past greatness, China is bound to begin flexing its muscles in the international arena. The wide gulf that separates our political system from that of China will continue to be a source of friction. Moreover, China has built up 150 years of resentment against the West. Now that China's leaders have an opportunity to reassert their influence in international affairs, we should expect confrontation, not cooperation. Given this reality, the United States should construct a barrier to Chinese expansion.

Considering trade-offs

•Will pressuring Beijing contribute to the breakdown of order in China, triggering an outpouring of tens of millions of Chinese refugees and setting the stage for a dangerous civil war?

•Will drawing a new dividing line in international relations leave American companies shut out of the fastest-growing market in the world and ultimately lead to a confrontation between the United States and East Asia?

•Will turning our back on democratic reformers in China undermine democratic movements throughout the world, especially in East Asia?

View 4 — Keep our distance

China is not the next frontier for democracy, nor is it a boundless market for U.S. exports, nor is it a hostile potential superpower. It is neither an irresistible opportunity nor a looming threat. Rather, China is a poor, struggling country that is far from our shores. As such, it should not rank as a leading concern for Americans. The United States must not allow U.S.-Chinese relations to distract our country from the enormous challenges we face here at home. If anything, we should take measures to protect American industries from the flood of cheap imports that are produced in China's sweatshops and prisons.

Considering trade-offs

•Will withdrawing from East Asia entice the expansionists in Beijing to fill the power vacuum, thus triggering a regional arms race?

•Will opening up new trade disputes with Beijing lead to deepening mistrust in U.S.-Chinese relations and ultimately harm American business interests in China?

•Will ignoring developments in China deprive Chinese reformers of vital support as their country undergoes a critical period of change?

Your turn

These views are by no means the only U.S. options. Rather, they are intended to lay out some of the most important values and assumptions underlying the debate on U.S. policy toward China and to spur discussion on the direction our country should take regarding this pressing issue. When you meet next time, you will have an opportunity to discuss U.S. policy toward China with others. The following statements are designed to help you clarify your thoughts on what is most important to you concerning this issue. Take a few moments to respond. This is a tool for you to get started. It will not be collected.

Rate each of the statements according to your beliefs:

1 = Strongly Support	3 = Oppose	5 = Undecided
2 = Support	4 = Strongly Oppose	

___ International stability and order should be protected because they are vital to the interests of the United States.

___ Only those countries that share our commitment to human rights and democracy can be counted among our most trustworthy allies.

___ Culture and geography largely determine which countries are enemies of the United States.

___ The United States has far more to fear from a weak, unstable China than from a strong, confident China.

___ Problems in the international arena are far less important for Americans than the challenges we face at home, such as poverty, crime, and budget deficits.

___ The interests of the United States can be maintained only if we resolutely exercise our power and influence in international affairs.

___ Involving ourselves in the affairs of other countries is wasteful and dangerous.

___ As Americans, we have the right and the responsibility to spread democracy around the world.

___ We will always have to compete with other leading nations for power.

Suggested reading

Fairbank, John King. *China: A New History* (Cambridge, Massachusetts: Harvard University Press, 1992).

Kristof, Nicholas D. and WuDunn, Sheryl. *China Wakes: The Struggle for the Soul of a Rising Power* (New York: Times Books, 1994).

Madsen, Richard. *China and the American Dream: A Moral Inquiry* (Berkeley, California: University of California Press, 1995).

Schell, Orville. *Mandate of Heaven: A New Generation of Entrepreneurs, Dissidents, Bohemians, and Technocrats Lays Claim to China's Future* (New York: Simon and Schuster, 1994).

Chapter 7

Shifting Sands: Balancing U.S. Interests in the Middle East

The U.S. Air Force's Prince Sultan Air Base lies deep in the barren desert of Saudi Arabia. Little more than half a century ago, the area knew only infrequent camel caravans. Today, it is marked by a 15,000-foot runway and barracks that house more than 4,000 American troops. Beyond the base's outer ring, a security perimeter extends a quarter mile into the desert. Guard units equipped with the latest night-vision technology track movements around the clock in the empty stretches of sand.

By any measure, the Prince Sultan Air Base is a remarkable feat of American engineering and ingenuity. At the same time, it raises important questions about our country's involvement in a part of the world that increasingly dominates U.S. foreign policy.

The air base is designed to protect U.S. interests in the Middle East. In

The Middle East in the American Century

The modern Middle East grew out of the devastation of World War I and the destruction of the Ottoman empire. Much of the most important wartime action took place away from the battlefield. In 1917, the British issued the "Balfour Declaration," pledging to help establish a "national home" for Jews in what were then the Ottoman provinces of Palestine. At the same time, the British won Arab support by promising their help in setting up an independent Arab state after the war. Away from public view, however, the British and French signed a secret treaty to carve up the Arab provinces of the Ottoman empire between themselves.

President Woodrow Wilson briefly posed an obstacle to their designs, but America's quick retreat from the international scene after the war left the two leading colonial powers free to complete the division of the defeated Ottoman empire. The British laid claim to the chief prizes, extending their influence to Mesopotamia (present-day Iraq and Kuwait), most of the Arabian peninsula, Palestine, and Transjordan (present-day Jordan). The French asserted control over what are today Syria and Lebanon.

By the early 1920s, the outlines of today's Middle East were clearly recognizable. With few changes, the map drawn by the Allies at the Paris Peace Conference was to remain intact. Britain's contradictory promises during World War I planted the seeds of the Arab-Israeli conflict. The heavy hand of European imperialism bred growing resentment against the West, giving rise to new political movements that stressed angry nationalism and a revival of Islam. On the economic front, the stage was set for the development of the oil industry in the Middle East.

Cold War rivalries

World War II brought down the old order of international relations and drew the United States into the Middle East as a major actor. With the decline of British power, the United States moved to counter the rising influence of the Soviet Union in the region. By 1948, U.S. policy in the Middle East was clearly framed by the Cold War, America's growing demand for

a crisis, U.S. pilots are positioned to provide air support for the more than 15,000 American troops stationed nearby. They are a few minutes flying time from the Persian Gulf — the center of the world's oil industry. Veering toward the north, U.S. pilots are within easy reach of Iraq and Iran, two countries that American leaders have identified as enemies of the United States. A few hundred miles to the west and U.S. warplanes are over Israel, a long-time ally of the United States and the flashpoint of four wars since 1948.

In 1991, 100 U.S. warplanes from the facilities at Prince Sultan took part in the huge multinational effort that defeated Iraqi dictator Saddam Hussein in the Persian Gulf War. In 1996, the air base was expanded after a suicide bombing attack on another U.S. installation in Saudi Arabia claimed the lives of nineteen American soldiers.

oil, and the establishment of Israel.

No country zoomed faster toward the top of the U.S. agenda than Saudi Arabia. Although Saudi oil production in the late 1940s was still meager, geologists had already estimated that the country contained the world's largest oil reserves. American executives of the Arabian-American Oil Company, known as Aramco, increasingly cooperated with U.S. foreign policymakers to shield the desert kingdom from outside threats.

America's efforts to outflank the Soviets in the Persian Gulf were complicated by the establishment of Israel. The Saudi royal family and most other Arab leaders opposed Zionism. Nonetheless, the United States played a key role in bringing the Jewish state into existence.

In 1947, a plan to divide Britain's mandate in Palestine between Jews and Palestinians passed the UN General Assembly by two votes, thanks in large part to American lobbying. With the withdrawal of the last British forces in May 1948, the state of Israel was proclaimed and immediately won recognition from the United States and the Soviet Union. Full-fledged fighting soon engulfed the former mandate. By the time a truce was reached in January 1949, the Jews had seized much of the land that the UN had designated for the Palestinians. More than 500,000 Palestinians became refugees.

Meanwhile, the politics of the Arab world underwent profound changes. Egypt's Gamal Abd al-Nasser emerged as the most prominent voice of Arab nationalism. He campaigned for pan-Arabism — the unification of Arabs into a single state. U.S. officials mistrusted Nasser but felt that his popularity could not be ignored. At the same time, they began to see Israel as a counterweight to expanding Soviet influence in Egypt, Syria, and Iraq. In 1962, President John Kennedy approved the sale of advanced anti-aircraft missiles to Israel, along with a loan to help the Israelis pay for their purchase. The arms sales marked the beginning of a steady flow of American military equipment to Israel.

In June 1967, overheated nationalism, growing superpower involvement, and an escalating arms build-up exploded into war

America's growing commitment in the Middle East is at odds with the overall direction of U.S. foreign policy. Since the collapse of the Soviet Union, the United States has been scaling back its international role. Without the pressure to contain Soviet communism, the U.S. defense budget has been cut. American troops have been withdrawn from overseas bases in Western Europe and elsewhere. Foreign aid spending in most parts of the world has been slashed. U.S. leaders — in step with the mood of the American public — have largely turned their attention to problems at home.

Two events help explain why the U.S. role in the Middle East has run counter to the trends of the 1990s.

First, the Persian Gulf War placed the United States at the center of the balance of power in the Middle East. In leading a coalition of twenty-eight nations, the United States succeeded in driving Iraq's invasion force out of

between Israel and its Arab neighbors. In a surprise attack, Israel destroyed most of the Egyptian and Syrian air forces on the ground. With control of the air, the Israeli army rolled across the Sinai to the Suez Canal, drove the Jordanian army out of the Old City of Jerusalem, overran the West Bank, and captured the strategic Golan Heights from Syria.

What came to be known as the Six-Day War again changed the map of the Middle East. Israel refused to withdraw from the territory it had conquered. Instead, the Israelis became responsible for governing more than 1 million Palestinians on the West Bank and the Gaza Strip. The Six-Day War also set the stage for the next round of fighting in the Middle East. Arab leaders were more determined than ever to match the military might of the Israelis. Increasingly, they turned to the Soviets for help.

For the United States, the so-called October War of 1973 brought America's chief concerns in the Middle East to the boiling point. In the first days of the war, the element of surprise belonged to Egypt and Syria. The Arab states also enjoyed an outpouring of military assistance from the Soviet Union. By the second week of fighting, the United States decided to do the same for Israel and began airlifting 1,000 tons of military supplies a day.

Oil and instability

Most significantly, the October War prompted Arab states to lead an oil embargo against the United States. At the same time, they reduced their overall production by 10 percent and vowed to lower oil output by 5 percent a month until Israel withdrew from the territories occupied in the 1967 War and restored the rights of the Palestinians.

The Arab measures set off an economic panic. Oil prices rose as high as $17 a barrel — six times the price in early October 1973. Gasoline prices in the United States jumped 40 percent. The oil embargo, however, failed to bend U.S. policy. Anwar Sadat, who succeeded Nasser in 1970, believed that continuing to pressure Washington would backfire. In March 1974, he convinced Arab leaders to lift the embargo.

While the October War was the most destructive conflict yet between Arabs and Israelis, it also laid the groundwork for the first steps toward peace. In 1978, President Jimmy

Kuwait. Nonetheless, Iraq's Saddam Hussein held on to power and has continued to defy the international community. The more than 4,000 U.S. troops at the Prince Sultan Air Base are there primarily because of the threat from Saddam.

Second, Israel and its Arab neighbors have taken the first steps toward achieving a peaceful settlement of their long conflict. Again, the initiative came from the United States. Since 1991, the United States has sponsored a series of peace talks. As a result, breakthrough agreements have been signed between Israel and the Palestinians, as well as between Israel and Jordan. The peace process, however, remains fragile, with all sides looking to the United States for leadership.

The shift in America's foreign policy resources toward the Middle East has taken place largely without significant debate. Unlike U.S. policy in

Carter initiated negotiations between Sadat and Israeli Prime Minister Menachem Begin that produced a peace treaty. In exchange for Israel's withdrawal from the Sinai Peninsula, Egypt became the first Arab country to recognize Israel.

While the Camp David accords brought Egypt securely into the U.S. camp, America's influence in Iran was challenged by a radical Islamist movement. By 1978, the efforts of the shah of Iran, Mohammed Reza Pahlavi, to channel his country's sudden oil wealth toward modernization and industrialization had bred deep resentment. Islamist leaders were in the best position to exploit the widening gulf between rich and poor in Iranian society. They orchestrated a wave of demonstrations that plunged the country into turmoil. After the shah left the country in January 1979, the spiritual leader of the Islamists, the Ayatollah Ruhollah Khomeini, embarked on a revolutionary agenda aimed at purging the country of Western popular culture. When Carter permitted the shah to enter the United States for medical treatment, Khomeini claimed that Washington was plotting a counter-revolution. In November 1979, Iranian students seized the U.S. embassy in Tehran. For over a year, they held the U.S. embassy staff as hostages.

The Iranian Revolution touched off another panic in the oil market. Again prices soared, nearly tripling in a few weeks. The crimp in oil supplies was compounded by fresh conflict in the Middle East. In the Persian Gulf, Saddam Hussein attacked Iran in hope of exploiting the confusion in the Iranian army. From 1980 to 1988, the war seesawed back and forth, claiming more than 1 million lives before an inconclusive cease-fire was reached. In Lebanon, fifteen years of civil war killed 150,000 people and drew in Syria, Israel, and the United States.

At the same time, the United States and other developed nations learned to live with the uncertainty of the Middle East's oil industry. The oil price hikes of the 1970s spurred energy conservation in wealthy countries. By 1983, oil consumption in the non-communist world had dropped by 11 percent from 1979 levels. Higher prices also led oil companies to develop new resources in the North Sea, Alaska, and other sites outside the Middle East. From $34 a barrel at the beginning of the 1980s, oil prices slid to around $18 a barrel by the end of the decade. ❑

Western Europe after World War II or toward the Soviet Union during the Cold War, America's position in the Middle East is not grounded on a public consensus. As we approach the 21st century, our country as a whole needs to address the same questions that until now have been the exclusive province of U.S. policymakers.

Which interests and values should undergird America's position in the Middle East? How should the region's enormous oil reserves and our country's close relationship with Israel figure into our calculations? What is the challenge presented to America by the growing importance of Islam in the politics of the Middle East?

SECTION 1

Persian Gulf War reshapes policy

On July 25, 1990, the U.S. ambassador to Iraq, April Glaspie, met with Iraqi leader Saddam Hussein at the presidential palace in Baghdad. Their conversation focused on Saddam's charge that Kuwait was pumping oil that rightfully belonged to Iraq from deposits along the Iraqi-Kuwaiti border. The Iraqi dictator also complained that Kuwait was holding down oil prices to slow his country's economic recovery.

Although U.S. relations with Saddam were hardly warm, Baghdad and Washington had often been brought together by common interests. During the 1980s, the United States had tacitly supported Iraq in its war against the Islamist regime in Iran. Thus, U.S. officials, including Glaspie, believed that the dialogue between them and their counterparts in Iraq was marked by mutual understanding, if not trust. When the American ambassador left her meeting with Saddam, she was under the impression that she had clearly warned him of the dangers of using force to resolve his dispute with Kuwait. Eight days later, 100,000 Iraqi troops poured across the desert border into Kuwait.

Iraq's invasion left President George Bush in an awkward position. Both as president and vice-president, he had viewed Saddam Hussein as a useful counterweight to Iran and Syria. By mid-1990, however, both Bush's outlook and the world had changed considerably.

Persian Gulf oil and Israel's security continued to head the list of U.S. concerns in the Middle East. But the third element — containing the influence of the Soviet Union — had faded. Under Mikhail Gorbachev, the Soviet

Union in the late 1980s had sought to build bridges to the West. The divisions of the Cold War had given way to a spirit of cooperation. Moreover, the Soviet Union itself was beginning to teeter under the weight of an ailing economy and political turmoil.

During the Cold War, Iraq had been a close ally of the Soviets. Strong American action against Iraq could have set off a wider international crisis. Within hours of Iraq's invasion of Kuwait, however, Gorbachev stopped arms shipments to Saddam and then joined the United States in supporting a UN Security Council resolution demanding Iraq's immediate withdrawal from Kuwait.

With the Soviets on his side, President Bush had an opportunity to steer the international system in a new direction. Bush spoke of erecting a "new world order" in which the leading powers would work together to prevent aggression and enforce the rule of law internationally. He intended to make Saddam's grab for Kuwait a test case. At the same time, America's traditional interests in oil and Israel continued to figure into Bush's calculations.

Exercising power and persuasion

Decisions made during the heat of the Persian Gulf crisis were to leave

Courtesy of the U.S. Navy

Defense Secretary Richard Cheney briefs the media during the Persian Gulf War while General Colin Powell and General Norman Schwarzkopf look on from the first row.

a lasting impact on U.S. policy in the Middle East. In the days immediately following Iraq's invasion of Kuwait, Bush's top priority was to prevent Saddam from seizing the oil fields of northeastern Saudi Arabia. Saddam's occupation of Kuwait had given him control of one-quarter of global oil reserves. Extending his reach 200 miles further into Saudi Arabia would have put nearly half of the world's oil in his grasp. Bush rushed American troops to the region to block the Iraqi army's path.

Once Saudi Arabia was protected, the president carefully built domestic and international support for stronger measures against Iraq. He first pushed for an economic blockade against Iraq. In November 1990, Bush won UN approval to use "all necessary means" to force Iraq out of Kuwait. A deadline was set — January 15, 1991 — for Iraq to withdraw from Kuwait.

Courtesy of the XVIII Airborne Corps History Office

A U.S. helicopter lands in Saudi Arabia in a training exercise prior to the Persian Gulf War.

In five months, the United States positioned 540,000 troops in Saudi Arabia. America's European allies and several Arab states contributed forces as well. Bush favored attacking Iraq quickly. He doubted that economic sanctions alone would pressure Saddam out of Kuwait.

The president also felt that the coalition of twenty-eight nations he had assembled would not hold together long. Particularly worrisome was Saddam Hussein's appeal in the Arab world. Saddam sought to rekindle the Arab nationalism that Gamal Abd al-Nasser had popularized. American officials feared that his message would deepen hostility toward the United States throughout the Middle East.

Within the United States, debate about how America should respond to Iraq's aggression was intense. Opposition to using force against Iraq was strong, especially from U.S. military leaders. Many warned that Iraq would turn to chemical weapons or international terrorism if attacked. There were worries that Iraq might even possess nuclear bombs. Others argued that economic sanctions should be given more time to take effect. When Bush asked the Senate to approve military action in early January 1991, his request passed by only five votes.

After the assault against Iraq began in mid-January 1991, Americans quickly rallied behind the war effort. Despite Saddam's prediction of "the mother of all battles," his army proved no match for the United States and its allies. For over a month, coalition warplanes pounded Iraqi targets with high-tech weaponry. By the time allied ground troops moved forward in late February 1991, communication links within Iraq's army had been shattered. Coalition forces retook Kuwait's capital, Kuwait City, with little resistance.

After 100 hours, Bush brought the ground war to a halt. The president objected to destroying Iraq's retreating army. Instead, he allowed what was left of Iraq's front-line divisions to limp northward.

The Persian Gulf War was one of the most lopsided conflicts in history. Iraq's military presented few obstacles to the advance of the coalition forces, while Iraqi missile attacks against Israel and Saudi Arabia caused minimal damage. Saddam Hussein inflicted his heaviest blow against the environment by ordering retreating Iraq troops to set hundreds of Kuwaiti oil wells on fire and to spill thousands of barrels of oil into the Persian Gulf.

In all, 146 American troops were killed during the war. (Coalition forces suffered a total of 260 deaths.) Iraq lost as many as 100,000 people, both soldiers and civilians, in the war.

Through a combination of power and persuasion, the United States had won greater influence in the Middle East. At the same time, there were fresh responsibilities. Once the fighting in the Persian Gulf ended, leaders in the region looked to the United States to maintain the new, American-made order.

SECTION 2

The geopolitics of oil

The Persian Gulf War passed without sparking another crisis in the oil market. Oil prices shot up in the days after Iraq's invasion of Kuwait, but soon settled back to their earlier levels.

Saudi Arabia acted to calm the world oil market during the troubles in the Persian Gulf. After the UN imposed an embargo on oil exports from Iraq and Iraqi-occupied Kuwait, the Saudis increased production to offset the

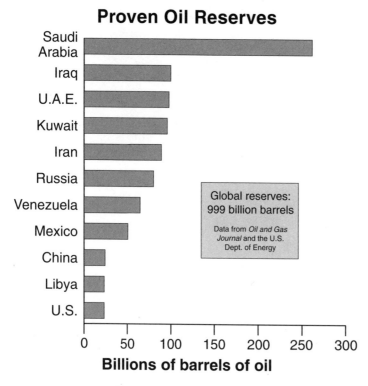

Proven Oil Reserves

Saudi Arabia

Iraq

U.A.E.

Kuwait

Iran

Russia

Venezuela

Mexico

China

Libya

U.S.

Global reserves:
999 billion barrels

Data from *Oil and Gas Journal* and the U.S. Dept. of Energy

0   50   100   150   200   250   300

Billions of barrels of oil

shortfall. By the mid-1990s, gasoline prices in the United States (taking inflation into account) had returned to levels not seen since before the 1973 oil embargo.

Long-term trends, however, are more doubtful. Worldwide, demand for oil in recent years has been growing at about 2 percent annually. The economic boom in East Asia has fueled much of the rise. In the United States, dependence on imported oil is creeping up as well.

With energy prices low, Americans are again buying more fuel-hungry cars and paying less attention to conservation. As a result, U.S. oil consumption has increased 10 percent since the mid-1980s. Meanwhile, U.S. oil production has dropped by about one-third since its peak in 1970. The United States today relies on the Middle East for about 10 percent of its oil needs. (Oil accounts for 38 percent of our country's total energy consumption.)

The Middle East remains the unrivalled center of the international oil industry. The region contains over 60 percent of the world's proven oil reserves. Most of the new fields that were discovered in the North Sea, Alaska, and elsewhere in the West after the 1973 oil crisis have passed their peak production years. Middle East oil is also the cheapest to pump. The cost of extracting a barrel of oil from the North Sea, for example, typically exceeds $10, compared to less than $2 a barrel in the Persian Gulf area. Many of America's key trading partners in Western Europe and East Asia rely on the region for the bulk of their oil.

But while the Middle East's oil resources loom larger than ever in the global economy, the likelihood of a repetition of the 1973 oil embargo seems distant. The Middle East's main oil exporters — Saudi Arabia, Kuwait, Iran, and Iraq — are sharply divided on both economic and political issues. As never before, the United States has come to play the role of policeman in the neighborhood.

The Middle East's economic clout has also faded. After the 1973 oil price hikes, the fortunes of the major oil exporters were on the rise. One by one, Middle Eastern leaders negotiated new deals with Western oil companies that gave their countries ownership of the oil under their lands. Huge profits transformed the Middle Eastern oil producers into international financial heavyweights.

Since the decline of oil prices in the mid-1980s, however, profit margins have shrunk. Ownership of the oil under their lands has not freed Middle Eastern countries from the constraints of the marketplace. Oil producers continue to depend mostly on Western oil companies to sell their product.

Oil's status in the world economy has slipped too. Today's most rapidly advancing economies are based primarily on manufacturing, not on raw materials. For example, Saudi Arabia generated $38 billion in oil exports in 1994. Taiwan, an East Asian country that imports virtually all of its oil, exported $93 billion worth of manufactured goods the same year.

Meanwhile, soaring populations, rising government expenditures, and arms imports have placed new financial pressures on Middle Eastern states.

Daily U.S. Oil Consumption

Figures are for thousands of barrels of oil.	Total Oil Consumption	Oil Imports from the Persian Gulf	Total Net Oil Imports
1995	17,725	1,573	7,886
1990	16,988	1,966	7,161
1985	15,726	311	4,286
1980	17,056	1,519	6,385
1975	16,322	1,165	5,846
1973	17,308	848	6,025

America's desert outpost

American presidents since Jimmy Carter have expressed their determination to go to war to prevent hostile forces from gaining control of the Middle East's oil resources. During the Cold War, America's tough talk was directed primarily against the Soviet Union and its allies. Today, the spotlight is on regional strongmen, such as Saddam Hussein.

Without the need to confront the Soviets in Europe, American defense strategists see the Persian Gulf as the most probable arena for future U.S. military action. The war against Iraq elevated the region's importance from the American perspective. It also convinced Saudi Arabia, Kuwait, and the smaller states of the Persian Gulf that an American military presence is needed in the region to safeguard their own security.

The presence of more than 15,000 American troops in the Persian Gulf, however, has created tensions of its own. Unlike in Western Europe, the

A U.S. soldier inspects a truck entering Prince Sultan Air Base.

Americans and the Arabs of the Persian Gulf share little in the way of common values and culture. Saudi Arabia and its five oil-rich neighbors in the Gulf Cooperation Council are ruled by iron-fisted royal families. Traditions run deep, and individual freedoms are limited. There are financial questions as well. Maintaining 100 warplanes, twenty warships, and heavily armored ground units costs about $70 billion a year. Although the Persian Gulf states pay part of the bill, the American portion represents a large chunk of the U.S. defense budget.

From the Arab standpoint, the U.S. military presence is a painful reminder of the Arab world's weaknesses and divisions. Along with the sudden wealth that oil has brought to the kingdoms of the Persian Gulf has come resentment from Arab neighbors. Kuwaitis, for example, received scant sympathy from most of the Arab world after their country was overrun by Iraq. At the time, most of the work in Kuwait was performed by more than 500,000 foreigners, nearly half of whom were Palestinian. Since Iraq's defeat, Kuwaitis have rebuilt in large part with labor from outside the Arab world, while counting on the United States for protection.

In addition to the physical presence of U.S. soldiers, the Middle East is also bristling with American weapons. The region is the world's largest market for arms exports, accounting for over half of the overseas sales of American companies. As the U.S. defense budget has shrunk, many American arms manufacturers have turned to the Middle East for new orders. In the next five years, the Persian Gulf states alone are expected to buy $75 billion worth of weapons.

SECTION 3

Friends and enemies

While concentrating on security issues, U.S. policymakers have paid much less attention to promoting democracy and human rights in the Middle East. In Latin America, the former Soviet Union, and other parts of the world, the United States often determines foreign aid, trade relations, and other aspects of foreign policy on the basis of political reform. In contrast, U.S. leaders have largely ignored what America's friends in the Middle East do within their borders.

The Arab kingdoms of the Persian Gulf present the most striking contradiction for U.S. policy. In Saudi Arabia, for example, women are not permitted to vote or even drive. Government and industry is dominated by the Saudi royal household, which numbers in the tens of thousands.

Other U.S. allies in the Middle East also remain tightly controlled from the top. Egypt's leadership, for example, deals harshly with local critics. Human rights groups complain that torture and imprisonment without trial are widespread. In Jordan, where King Hussein has opened up the political process in recent years, democracy still seems a distant goal.

Turkey is a special case, but in its own way equally troubling. Since the collapse of the Ottoman empire, Turkey has emerged as the most Westernized Muslim country in the Middle East. Democratic institutions have gained acceptance among the people, while Islam's influence on government policy has been curbed.

Yet, Turkey's image has been scarred by the ethnic divisions within the country. Turkey is home to roughly 12 million Kurds, an ancient people of the Middle East. Until 1991, the use of the Kurdish language or even acknowledging the existence of the Kurds was illegal. Today, Kurdish organizations of any kind are prohibited. With no political outlets to express their concerns, Kurdish groups have waged a low-scale guerrilla war in Turkey's southeast since 1984. The conflict has claimed more than 23,000 lives and left most of the region subject to emergency rule.

Turkey's civil war and the hard-line rule of most Arab states have contributed to the Middle East's reputation for instability. For U.S. policymakers, the chief fear is that shaky regimes will give way to pressure for radical change and make the region still more dangerous for the United States.

Enemies list

U.S. policy in the Middle East has been defined as much by our country's enemies as by our friends. Since the Persian Gulf War, America's main foes in the region have been Iran and Iraq.

In U.S. eyes, Iran and Iraq (along with Libya) are classified as "rogue states," or international outlaws. The charges against them are extensive. Iraq, and possibly Iran, have sought to develop nuclear weapons. Their stockpiles of chemical weapons are substantial. Both countries have also tried to dominate the Persian Gulf either through military force or political meddling. American officials contend that Iran and Iraq are key sponsors of international terrorism.

In the 1990s, U.S. policy in the Middle East has been geared toward containing the influence of Iran and Iraq. American constraints on Iraq have been comparatively straight-forward.

In the aftermath of the Persian Gulf War, President Bush backed away from pursuing the overthrow of Saddam Hussein's regime after Saudi Arabia and Turkey voiced concern that Iraq's disintegration would destabilize the region. Instead, Bush blocked Saddam from rebuilding his country's power and hoped that disgruntled military officers would eventually bring about a change in government.

At American urging, the UN Security Council has strictly limited Saddam Hussein's freedom to maneuver. Many of the economic sanctions that were imposed on Iraq in 1990 have been maintained. Saddam still cannot sell his country's oil freely on the international market. The UN has prohibited the Iraqi air force from flying over northern and southern Iraq. U.S., British, and French pilots have enforced the no-fly zones. In addition, UN monitors conduct regular inspections of Iraq to prevent Saddam from acquiring nuclear weapons.

Keeping the squeeze on Iraq, however, has placed strains on U.S. foreign policy. Repeatedly, the United States has responded to Iraqi violations of UN agreements by launching air strikes or rushing additional troops to

© Bruce Beattie. Copley News Service

"On second thought, maybe you SHOULD get rid of Saddam Hussein...oh, and take out the garbage. That will be all."

the region. Economic sanctions have not brought about Saddam's downfall. Rather, they have prompted accusations that the United States is aggravating the suffering of the Iraqi people. According to estimates by the UN, 4,500 Iraqi children die each month because of malnutrition and disease attributable to the sanctions. Such reports have fractured the unity of the Persian Gulf War coalition.

U.S. steps to contain Iran have provoked stronger international criticism, largely because the United States has acted alone. In 1995, the United States prohibited Americans from trading with or investing in Iran. The sanctions cost an American energy company, Conoco, a $1 billion deal to develop Iranian oil and natural gas fields.

In 1996, the United States tried to persuade foreign countries to cut their business ties to Iran and Libya with a more restrictive set of sanctions. Under the new measure, foreign companies that invest more than $20 million annually in the energy industries of Iran or Libya would be banned from access to American markets and loans from American banks.

Most U.S. allies have criticized the sanctions and have continued to do business with Iran and Libya. A French company, for example, stepped in to fill the gap left by Conoco. U.S. officials, however, contend that the sanctions have slowed the flow of investment into Iran. They argue that Iran's government could be tamed if, in particular, Western European countries joined in squeezing Iran economically.

Political Islam

The Iranian Revolution brought to the forefront a new concern for Washington: the appeal of Islamist political movements. In almost all Middle Eastern countries, Islam is officially recognized as the binding force of society. State-run television and radio stations broadcast thousands of hours of religious programming, and Islamic clergymen receive government salaries. The Islamist regimes of Iran and Sudan, however, take a more radical approach. There, the Islamic clergy actually controls the government.

Political Islam — or Islamic fundamentalism as it is often called — strives to establish Islamic law as the foundation of government and to rid society of non-Islamic influences. Political Islam has fed off the frustration of Middle Eastern politics in the 20th century. Earlier movements, such as pan-Arab nationalism, have been branded as failures. Corruption and inefficiency have undermined popular faith in government.

Islamist movements have benefited from larger economic and social forces as well. In the 1990s, many Middle Eastern countries have adopted free-market economic principles advocated by the United States. The reforms call for breaking down trade barriers that have protected local industries, cutting government spending, and selling off state-run companies to private owners. While free-market policies have attracted increased foreign investment to the Middle East, they have also raised unemployment and reduced government assistance to the poor.

Islamic movements have proven especially strong in the poor neighborhoods of large cities. Many of their supporters are recent migrants from the countryside or the victims of economic reform. For them, Islamist movements are an answer to the seemingly reckless change and economic inequity they see around them.

U.S. officials and many Middle Eastern leaders see political Islam as a threat. In Egypt, for example, Washington has stood behind Egyptian President Hosni Mubarak's crackdown on Islamist political movements. The situation in Algeria has been much more violent. In 1992, the Algerian military cancelled elections that were expected to bring an Islamist political party to power. Divisions within Algeria quickly sharpened, igniting a fierce civil war that has killed more than 50,000 Algerians. Since elections were held in 1995, the United States has backed the Algerian government's efforts to restore order.

In Turkey, Jordan, and Yemen, Islamist parties have been allowed to participate in the political process. In 1996, Necmettin Erbakan became Turkey's first Islamist prime minister after his Welfare Party won the largest share of the vote in parliamentary elections. Erbakan's support for religious education prompted sharp criticism from the Turkish military, bringing down his coalition in parliament. The two sides, however, agreed to give the last word to Turkey's voters.

Meanwhile, the Iranian Revolution that first set off alarm bells about political Islam has itself lost much of its fire. Since the death of Khomeini in 1989, Iran's leadership has been less eager to export its revolution abroad. Iran's military budget amounts to only one-sixth of Saudi Arabia's and one-half of Israel's. Iran has also taken steps to encourage foreign investment. The election of a moderate, Mohammed Khatami, as president in May 1997 suggests that Iranian voters want to soften the Iranian Revolution.

The record of Iran's Islamic Republic presents a contradictory picture. The clergymen who lead the country continue to involve the state in the private lives of their citizens. They enforce Islamic dress codes that require women to cover themselves in public. They have also outlawed satellite dishes that had been used to pick up Iranian-language television programming beamed from California.

Most Iranians, however, are better off under the Islamic Republic than they were under the shah. Life expectancy in the country has risen from 55 years in the late 1970s to 68 years today. Schools, health clinics, roads, and safe drinking water have been brought to remote villages neglected by the shah.

Under Islamic law, the rights of women in Iran are restricted. They cannot travel abroad without the permission of their husbands and their testimony in court is worth half that of a man. Nonetheless, Iranian women as a whole have made progress since the fall of the shah and are clearly ahead of their counterparts in most of the Arab kingdoms of the Persian Gulf. For example, 40 percent of the students in Iranian universities are women, and 95 percent of girls attend primary school.

SECTION 4

Arab-Israeli peace prospects

Along with the rest of the Middle East, the assumptions of the main actors in the Arab-Israeli conflict were shaken by the Persian Gulf War. The handful of long-range Iraqi missiles that struck Israel during the war reinforced the country's vulnerability. Moreover, Israelis increasingly viewed the occupation of the West Bank and Gaza Strip as a burden on their society, especially after Palestinians launched a broad-based protest movement in 1987.

For the Palestinians, PLO Chairman Yasir Arafat's decision to back Saddam Hussein seriously backfired. The Arab kingdoms of the Persian Gulf punished Arafat by cutting off funding for the PLO. Hundreds of thousands of Palestinian workers were no longer welcome in Kuwait after the Persian Gulf War. The collapse of the Soviet Union also deprived the Palestinians of another key source of support in the international arena.

Jordan's King Hussein reluctantly backed Saddam Hussein as well, largely to avoid provoking the Palestinian community that makes up a majority of Jordan's population. After the war, the king had no choice but to mend his fences with the United States.

Syria's prestige rose as a result of the war. Syrian President Hafez al-Assad joined the international coalition against his bitter rival, Saddam Hussein. Although U.S. officials were suspicious of Assad's motives, they were eager for closer relations with Syria to tighten the noose around Saddam.

Finally, the Persian Gulf War boosted the leverage of the United States. President Bush decided to use America's enhanced image to try once again to achieve peace between Israel and its Arab neighbors. In October 1991, he persuaded representatives of Israel, the Palestinians, Syria, Jordan, and Lebanon to sit down together in Madrid. The participants at the Madrid conference recognized that the Arab-Israeli conflict was not likely to be resolved with a single treaty. Rather, separate peace talks were initiated between Israel and each of its Arab neighbors.

Israeli-Palestinian agreements

Negotiations between the Israelis and the Palestinians have achieved the most significant breakthroughs. In 1993, Israeli Prime Minister Yitzhak Rabin and PLO Chairman Arafat shook hands on the White House lawn to seal their first agreement. In the declaration of principles they signed, Israel accepted the PLO as the legitimate representative of the Palestinian people while the PLO recognized Israel's right to exist in peace and security, and renounced the use of violence. Both sides expressed their support

Courtesy of the White House

President Clinton joins Israeli Prime Minister Rabin and PLO Chairman Arafat as they seal their 1993 peace treaty with a handshake on the White House lawn.

for earlier UN resolutions, which called on Israel to withdraw from territories it had occupied in exchange for an Arab commitment to peaceful relations.

In 1995, Rabin and Arafat again met at the White House to sign a much more detailed treaty. The second agreement laid out a plan to extend Palestinian self-rule in the West Bank and to bring Israel's military occupation of the area to a close.

The treaties between Israel and the PLO have produced concrete changes. A Palestinian government, called the Palestinian Authority, largely runs day-to-day affairs in half the Gaza Strip and the main cities of the West Bank, except East Jerusalem. For the first time, Palestinians manage their own police force and elect the officials that govern them.

Many of the thorniest issues, however, have yet to be resolved by Israeli and Palestinian negotiators. Above all, the Palestinians insist on attaining full statehood. They want to control their own borders, form an army, and exercise the other rights belonging to independent nations. The Israelis fear that a full-fledged Palestinian state will endanger their security. They argue that an independent Palestine could be used as a staging ground for attacks against Israel. In fact, Israeli forces continue to exercise sole authority over two-thirds of the West Bank.

The status of Jerusalem is another sticking point. Israel claims complete control over Jerusalem and since 1980 has made the city its capital. (The United States and most other nations do not recognize Jerusalem as Israel's capital.) The Palestinians, however, want to establish their capital in East Jerusalem, where they represent a majority of the population.

Like the status of Jerusalem, controversy over Jewish settlements in the West Bank and Gaza Strip has stirred passions. Roughly 145,000 Israelis live in the occupied territories. Most of them make their homes in modern suburbs ringing Jerusalem. Israeli construction in the area has continued despite the peace treaties. Other Israelis have settled in more remote areas, often for religious reasons. Many settlers vow that they will never accept Palestinian authority.

More than 2.2 million Palestinians live in the West Bank and Gaza Strip (an area the size of Delaware). As many as 3 million other Palestinians live scattered throughout the Arab world, mostly in Jordan. Palestinian leaders argue that all Palestinians — many of whom were forced to flee by the 1967 War — should have the right to live in the West Bank and Gaza Strip. Israeli authorities have resisted opening the occupied territories to unrestricted immigration. They worry that an influx of immigrants would further inflame the West Bank and Gaza Strip. Israelis also note that more than 850,000 Palestinians live within Israel's borders.

Israeli and Palestinian negotiators are scheduled to conclude a final agreement by May 1999. Political developments in the region, however, have cast both the deadline and the entire peace process in doubt. In 1995, Israeli Prime Minister Rabin was gunned down by an Israeli extremist. His assassination created an opening for Benjamin Netanyahu, a strong critic of the peace process. In 1996, Netanyahu was narrowly elected prime minister.

Meanwhile, Rabin's partner in the peace process, PLO Chairman Arafat, faces challenges of his own. Many Palestinians have grown frustrated under the Palestinian Authority. Most have slipped economically in the 1990s, as the Israeli government has reduced their access to job opportunities within Israel. Corruption and mismanagement by the Palestinian Authority have further shaken the confidence of Palestinians in their leadership.

Palestinian disappointment has generated support for hard-line Islamist militants who seek to derail the peace process through terrorism. In turn, Israel has demanded that Arafat clamp down on the militants. Israeli leaders have also been quick to order air strikes against suspected guerrilla bases in Lebanon.

Both Israelis and Palestinians concede that the United States plays the pivotal role in resolving their conflict. In addition to playing host at negotiating sessions, the United States has supported the peace process through foreign aid and diplomatic pressure.

Israel has long been the leading recipient of U.S. foreign aid, taking in $3 billion a year. (Egypt ranks second with $2.1 billion a year.) Since the 1993 greement, the United States has pledged $500 million in assistance for the alestinians over five years. At the same time, the United States has rallied international support for the peace process.

Uneasy neighbors

While Israeli-Palestinian peace talks have grabbed most of the headlines, other dimensions of the Arab-Israeli conflict are also important. Most noteworthy has been the signing of a peace treaty between Israel and Jordan in 1994. Under the agreement, Jordan joined Egypt in officially recognizing Israel. No other Arab state has yet to formally extend diplomatic relations to Israel, although Israel has established low-level ties with Morocco, Tunisia, Oman, and Qatar.

Resolving the Israeli-Syrian dispute remains crucial to lasting peace in the Middle East. Syrian President Assad has insisted that he will sign a peace treaty only if Israel returns the Golan Heights, which has been under Israeli occupation since the 1967 War. Israeli leaders have indicated their willingness to return at least part of the Golan Heights. However, the two sides remain divided over how much of the territory should be off-limits to the Syrian military.

Peace between Lebanon and Israel hinges on progress in Israeli-Syrian negotiations. Since the 1980s, Syria and Israel have each maintained a military presence in Lebanon. Assad claims that the more than 30,000 Syrian troops stationed in the eastern part of the country have helped quell Lebanon's civil war. Israeli leaders contend that the security zone they occupy in southern Lebanon is needed to protect their country against guerrilla attacks. As recently as 1996, they mounted a large-scale bombardment of guerrilla positions in southern Lebanon that forced 500,000 Lebanese civilians to temporarily flee their homes.

America's perspective

The Arab-Israeli peace process has commanded a greater share of America's diplomatic energy than any other issue in recent years. At the same time, it has raised new questions about U.S.-Israeli relations.

Since its creation, Israel has occupied a special position in U.S. foreign policy. Israeli interests have been effectively promoted in the United States by the lobbying efforts of America's influential Jewish community. U.S. leaders, however, have stood by Israel for other reasons as well.

First, Israel has won admiration in the United States as a model of democracy and Western values in the Middle East. Presidents Harry Truman and Lyndon Johnson were particularly committed to Israel's struggle for survival.

Other presidents, such as Richard Nixon and George Bush, viewed Israel primarily as a strategic ally in the region. They valued Israel for countering U.S. enemies in the Middle East, battle testing U.S. weapons, and sharing intelligence information. Israel's development of nuclear weapons (which Israeli officials have never admitted) gave Israel added weight.

With the end of the Cold War and the evolution of Israel's position in the Middle East, America's attachment to Israel has attracted fresh attention. Israel's heavy-handed treatment of the Palestinians under its jurisdiction and repeated incursions into southern Lebanon have drawn more intense criticism. Under President Bill Clinton, however, U.S. support for Israel has not wavered.

Section 5

Views on U.S. options

Now that you have read about some of the issues related to U.S. policy toward the Middle East, it is time to take a closer look at what our country's position should be. In this section, you will explore four views on U.S. policy toward the Middle East. As you will see, each of the views is based on a distinct set of values and beliefs, and is shaped by a well-defined perspective on the threats and opportunities facing the United States.

The views presented address three fundamental questions that frame the discussion on U.S. policy toward China:

• **Should economic interests, particularly with respect to oil, dominate U.S. policy toward the Middle East?** Should U.S. policy be geared toward protecting access to Middle Eastern oil for ourselves and our main trading partners? Or should U.S. interests in the region emphasize our special relationship with Israel, the containment of anti-American regimes, and other conventional security concerns?

• **Should the United States seek to promote Western values in the Middle East?** Should the United States take advantage of its influence and prestige to press for wider acceptance of Western values, such as democracy, tolerance, free-market economic principles, human rights, and equality for women? Or should the United States respect the distinctiveness of the

Middle East's religious and cultural traditions and avoid involvement in the internal affairs of the region's governments?

•**Should the United States be prepared to intervene militarily in the Middle East to protect our country's vital interests?** Should the United States make it clear in the Middle East — just as we have in Western Europe, the Korean peninsula, and elsewhere — that we will respond with force to serious threats against vital U.S. interests? Or should the United States exercise military power in the region only when our country is directly threatened?

Each of the four views that follows responds differently to these questions. You should think of the views as a tool designed to help you examine the contrasting strategies from which Americans must define our country's role in the world and craft future policy.

View 1 — Eye on the prize

As Americans, we have no choice but to recognize our dependence on oil, and in particular on oil from the Middle East. As the events of the 1970s illustrated, a disruption in Middle Eastern oil supplies has the potential to send shockwaves throughout the global economy. In the face of such a threat, it should be clear that the flow of oil from the Middle East is vital to our country's prosperity and security. U.S. policy in the Middle East must be focused on ensuring that our country and our allies have access to the region's oil resources. Economic common sense demands that we take a more balanced approach toward the Arab-Israeli conflict. Likewise, there is no benefit in picking fights with Saddam Hussein or carrying out a crusade against imagined threats from Islamist movements.

Considering trade-offs

•Will abandoning sanctions against Iran and Iraq and turning our back on Israel be seen throughout the Middle East as a victory for America's enemies and a defeat for the United States?

•Will ignoring the brutality and corruption of oil-rich regimes tarnish America's international reputation as a force for democracy and freedom and embolden them to crack down on their opponents at home and bully their neighbors?

•Will focusing our country's resources on protecting the oil supplies of the Middle East distract us from the more important goal of developing new sources of energy here at home?

View 2 — *Policing a rough neighborhood*

Americans must accept that our country's strength and influence present an irresistible target for the Middle East's hate-mongers and extremists. We must also recognize that the region is too important to walk away from. There is no hope of compromise with fanatics who despise our values and our way of life. To protect our country's interests in the Middle East, the United States must draw a clear line in the sand. On one side belong our trusted friends and allies in the region. When their security is threatened, either by enemies beyond their borders or within, we should stand beside them. On the other side are the forces that have aligned themselves against peace and stability. They must be contained.

Considering trade-offs

• Will carrying out a crusade against Iraq, Iran, and Libya leave the United States isolated from the rest of the international community and cost American companies opportunities for business?

• Will branding Islamist leaders as our enemies only provoke deeper feelings of hostility toward the United States within the Muslim world and draw America's resources away from urgent problems here at home?

• Will continued support for corrupt, undemocratic regimes in the Middle East discourage political and economic reform.?

View 3 — *Promote Western values*

In the past decade, the world has changed for the better. The Middle East, however, has been a stubborn exception to the global trend. Politically, democracy has made scant headway in the region, especially in the Arab world. Basic freedoms and the rule of law count for little. Regrettably, U.S. policy has contributed to the Middle East's lack of progress. For too many years, we have put our oil interests and security concerns ahead of principle. The time has come for the United States to use its enormous influence in the Middle East to nudge the region toward reform. For the United States to bring reform to the Middle East, our policies must be seen as fair and even-handed. Change for the better is possible in the region, but only if our country leads the way.

Considering trade-offs

• Will trying to impose American values on cultures that are distinctly different from our own only contribute to further hostility toward the United

States and expose our country to charges of upholding a double standard?

• Will forcing Middle Eastern countries to adopt reckless reforms lead to the downfall of many of our friends and allies, deepen poverty, and play into the hands of extremists?

• Will picking fights with countries that control a large share of the world's oil reserves undermine America's vital economic interests in the Middle East?

View 4 — Break free of entanglements

America's foreign policy chessmasters and armchair military strategists may have turned the Middle East into their latest field of play, but for the rest of us heightened U.S. involvement in the region is a costly, dangerous adventure. The United States must break free of our country's entanglements in the Middle East. The military presence that we have built up in recent years must be removed before we find ourselves caught up in another war. We can no longer allow our country to serve as a convenient target for anti-American extremists. Likewise, we should not be held responsible for guaranteeing peace between Arabs and Israelis. U.S. relations with the countries of the Middle East should be limited to the economic issues that matter most to Americans.

Considering trade-offs

• Will withdrawing America's military from the Middle East open the door to new aggression against the oil-rich states of the Persian Gulf, set off an even more dangerous arms race, and increase the likelihood that nuclear weapons will spread in the region?

• Will turning our back on the Middle East remove one of the few forces for positive change in the region?

• Will walking away from the Arab-Israeli peace process lead to a breakdown in negotiations and another round of fighting in the region?

Your turn

These views are by no means the only U.S. options. Rather, they are intended to lay out some of the most important values and assumptions underlying the debate on U.S. policy toward Middle East and to spur discussion on the direction our country should take regarding this pressing issue. When you meet next time, you will have an opportunity to discuss U.S. policy toward the Middle East with others. The following statements are designed to help you clarify your thoughts on what is most important to you concerning this issue. Take a few moments to respond. This is a tool for you to get started. It will not be collected.

Rate each of the statements according to your beliefs:

1 = Strongly Support   3 = Oppose   5 = Undecided

2 = Support   4 = Strongly Oppose

____ Political disputes and cultural differences should not prevent Americans from doing business with all countries.

____ U.S foreign policy should be directed toward promoting American values in other countries.

____ International stability and order should be protected because they are vital to the interests of the United States.

____ Economic interests should be the driving force behind U.S. foreign policy.

____ We should rely less on military force and other conventional foreign policy tools to solve the problems of today's interconnected world.

____ Questions of morality should not determine our relations with other countries.

____ Problems in the international arena are far less important for Americans than the challenges we face at home, such as poverty, crime, and budget deficits.

____ All countries are capable of making progress toward democracy, freedom, and tolerance.

____ America's enemies can be contained only if we remain strong and vigilant.

Suggested reading

Friedman, Thomas L. *From Beirut to Jerusalem* (New York: Anchor Books, Doubleday, 1995).

Lewis, Bernard. *The Middle East: A Brief History of the Last 2,000 Years* (New York: Scribner, 1995).

Said, Edward W. *Orientalism* (New York: Vintage Books, 1979).

Yergin, Daniel. *The Prize: The Epic Quest for Oil, Money, and Power* (New York: Simon and Schuster, 1991).

Chapter 8

U.S. Immigration Policy in an Unsettled World

Like no other major American city, Miami brings home the debate over the impact of immigration on the United States. Before 1959, Miami was a quiet town best known for its nearby beaches and popularity among snowbelt retirees. Then a communist revolution in Cuba brought an influx of Cubans fleeing persecution by the government of Fidel Castro. In the 1970s, the Cubans were joined by newcomers from Haiti. The 1980s witnessed a surge of Central and South American immigrants. By 1992, 60 percent of Miami residents had been born outside the United States and nearly three-quarters spoke a language other than English at home.

In Miami's *Calle Ocho* district, fruit and vegetable stalls sell black beans, guayabas, plantains, and papayas. Sidewalk vendors serve up *empanadas* and *quesadillas* filled with meat, fish, and cheese. Dominoes is the game of choice at the city park. Signs in Spanish advertise legal services, eye care,

Immigration in American History

The nation's early leaders said little about immigration and citizenship in the constitution, other than to make these issues the responsibility of Congress. Before 1820, the United States did not even bother to count how many newcomers reached its shores. For most of the 1800s, a nearly ideal balance existed between the problems of Europe and the needs of the United States. In Europe, the Industrial Revolution, shifts in agriculture, and a soaring population left millions unable to make a living. Meanwhile, the United States expanded in both size and wealth. The turn of the century, however, marked a major change in how immigrants fit into their adopted country. Rather than pushing the American frontier westward, they answered the call for cheap, unskilled labor in industrial cities. By 1900, four out of five New Yorkers either were born abroad or were the children of immigrants.

Restrictions on immigration

Anxiety about the social and political implications of immigration dates from the earliest days of the republic. It was not until the 1840s, however, that the first organized opposition to open immigration emerged. The American Party, better known as the Know-Nothing Party for the secretiveness of its members, claimed that Catholic immigrants, mainly of Irish and German origin, threatened to corrupt the country's heritage. Party members were behind violence to terrorize newcomers.

While the Know-Nothings faded from the political arena before the Civil War, an anti-immigration movement at the turn of the century revived many of the party's ideas. Labor union organizers feared that abundant cheap labor would undercut their struggle. Political reformers believed that immigrant voters would be manipulated to support corrupt politicians. Consequently, both groups supported the movement. Business leaders, however, opposed the campaign to restrict immigration.

The Chinese Exclusion Act of 1882 marked

hair styling, and political candidates. As a result of the city's transformation, Miami has emerged as an important crossroads in trade between the United States and Latin America. It has also become a hotbed of ethnic tension. Riots have erupted in Miami three times since 1980. The American-born population of the city actually fell by 90,000 in the 1980s.

What Miami represents to Americans is crucial to the future of U.S. immigration policy. For some, the city embodies what is best in America. In a few decades, newcomers have made it an international financial center — a gateway to the world poised to compete in the global economy of the 21st century. For others, Miami is a symbol of unbridled change, where differences in language and culture point to a future of economic conflict and social discord.

As Americans sort out the priorities that will set the tone of U.S. immigration laws, they will have to clarify their vision for America in the 21st

the first significant legislation to restrict immigration. In 1921, another restrictive law was passed, creating immigration quotas on the basis of national origin. That concept served as the foundation of the Immigration Act of 1924, commonly known as the National Origins Act.

The National Origins Act limited the number of immigrants accepted from each country by capping annual immigration of each European nationality at 2 percent of its proportion in the U.S. population in 1890. For groups that had begun immigrating to the United States in large numbers after 1890, such as Italians and Poles, the quotas were relatively small. Moreover, the 1924 act affirmed earlier laws that closed the door to immigration from Asia. From 1924 to 1952, immigration fell to its lowest level since the mid-1800s.

The onset of the Cold War in the late 1940s left its mark on U.S. immigration law. The new international position of the United States became evident in the Displaced Persons Act of 1948, which provided for the admission of more than 400,000 refugees from World War II. A number of special bills designed to accommodate "escapees" from communist domination followed in the 1950s and 1960s.

1965 opens a new era

The civil rights movement forced lawmakers to re-examine the national origins quotas and adopt a historic immigration reform bill. The Immigration and Nationality Act of 1965 replaced the old quotas with seven preference categories that gave priority to reuniting families and attracting skilled professionals. The act opened the door to unprecedented numbers of Asian doctors, engineers, scientists, and other university-trained specialists. It also allowed immigrants with citizenship status to sponsor the immigration of their spouses, children, and siblings. By the 1970s, immigrants were entering the United States in the largest numbers in half a century. ❑

century. We will have to weigh the impact of immigration on Miami, Los Angeles, New York, and other major cities that receive the great majority of our country's newcomers. As a nation, can we afford to continue absorbing immigrants at the current record rate? Conversely, can we afford to close our doors to their talents and skills? And what of the social implications? Do high rates of immigration tear at the cultural fabric of our society by aggravating ethnic, racial, and religious divisions? Or does the continued vibrancy of our nation of immigrants in fact depend on the new cultures and perspectives that newcomers bring with them?

As we consider this topic, we must recognize that the debate over immigration policy has expanded to incorporate a broad range of foreign policy issues. The current discussion touches on U.S. relations with Latin America, human rights, international trade, and the worldwide refugee crisis. This chapter will help prepare you to consider these issues.

SECTION 1

Assessing the impact of immigration

Economic concerns typically dominate the immigration debate. For most of this century, business leaders and big farmers have tended to favor open immigration policies to ensure an adequate supply of workers. Although opportunities for unskilled factory workers have declined since World War II, other businesses, such as hotels and restaurants, continue to depend on low-wage labor.

Supporters of open immigration also note that many high-tech industries have come to rely on newcomers. About one-quarter of immigrant workers are college graduates. Many have degrees in engineering, computer science, chemistry, and other fields that are in demand. Moreover, immigrants often retain connections to potential export markets. Immigrants from East Asia, for example, have contributed substantially to U.S. trade with the vibrant economies of that region.

Immigrant entrepreneurship has been felt most notably in America's biggest cities. During the past two decades, immigrants have helped revive downtown business districts by opening up small businesses, creating new jobs, and strengthening the local tax base.

Opposition to open immigration laws has come historically from labor union leaders who claim that high levels of immigration have taken away jobs from native-born Americans. They also maintain that the flow of unskilled workers into the economy holds down wages at the bottom of the employment ladder. Other critics argue that U.S. immigration policy drains poor countries of their most highly educated professionals. Officials in some poor countries have even made the case that they should be compensated by the United States for the highly skilled emigrants who leave their nations.

Social services

The expansion of government social service programs has added another dimension to the immigration debate. Although studies indicate that immigrants are not much more likely to receive welfare than the general population, many often need special help in education and health care during the first few years after their arrival. This has placed a substantial burden on a few regions. In 1996, for example, six states — California, New York, Texas, Florida, New Jersey, and Illinois — received 68 percent of all immigrants. California was the destination of 35 percent of immigrants during the 1980s. According to California Governor Pete Wilson, the latest wave of immigrants drains more resources from the state than it contributes. Wilson attributes California's budget deficit in part to the cost of education, health care, law enforcement, and welfare for immigrants. Similar expenses have strained other areas. In the state of Washington, for example, 9 percent of students come from homes in which English is not the family's native language.

Top Ten States of Intended Residence for Immigrants
(1996)

State	Number of immigrants	Percentage of total	State	Number of immigrants	Percentage of total
California	201,529	22.0%	*Illinois*	42,517	4.6%
New York	154,095	16.8%	*Massachusetts*	23,085	2.5%
Texas	83,385	9.1%	*Virginia*	21,375	2.3%
Florida	79,461	8.7%	*Maryland*	20,732	2.3%
New Jersey	63,303	6.9%	*Washington*	18,833	2.1%

Reprinted from the *1994 Statistical Yearbook of the INS*

Population trends

The concentration of immigrants in a handful of states has also raised questions about the relationship between immigration policy and population trends. In California, for example, the state's population grew 20 percent during the 1980s. Immigrants accounted for more than one-quarter of that increase. Like other countries in the developed world, the United States has experienced a drop in birth rates for most of this century. If immigration were closed off entirely, the U.S. population would actually begin falling around the year 2020. At current levels of immigration, however, the population is expected to reach 335 million by the year 2025 — an increase of 60 million people.

SECTION 2

The challenge of immigration reform

Immigration to the United States is currently at record levels. The 9.5 million newcomers who came in the 1980s surpassed the previous peak decade of U.S. immigration, from 1901 to 1910. (Immigrants at the turn of the century comprised 11.5 percent of America's population, as compared to 4.2 percent in the 1980s.) In 1996, roughly 1.2 million immigrants arrived in the United States. Of that total, 596,000 were relatives of U.S. citizens and permanent residents, 117,000 were skilled workers and their families, and 129,000 were refugees and asylum seekers. In addition, the Immigration and Naturalization Service (INS) estimated that 300,000 illegal aliens settled in the country. Since the mid-1970s, the United States has accepted more immigrants than the rest of the world's countries combined.

The current wave of new arrivals is the most highly educated group of immigrants in U.S. history. In the 1980s alone, 1.5 million college-educated newcomers joined the work force. Immigration patterns in recent decades have also brought the United States greater ethnic diversity. Between 1971 and 1991, more than 35 percent of legal immigrants came from Asia, while almost half arrived from Latin America, including 24 percent from Mexico. Fewer than 14 percent emigrated from Europe.

Changes in immigration law

The upsurge in immigration that began around 1970 follows a lull of nearly half a century. Much of the initial impetus is attributable to the landmark

Immigration and Nationality Act of 1965. In the past two decades, concern over lax border control, demands for changes in admission standards, and an upswing in refugee applications have prodded Congress to regularly revisit the issue of immigration policy. From 1980 to 1990, three major pieces of immigration legislation were enacted.

The Refugee Act of 1980 was prompted in large part by the arrival of more than 400,000 refugees from Southeast Asia between 1975 and 1980. The legislation sought to give refugee policy greater consistency by allowing for both a regular flow of refugees and emergency admissions. In 1986, the Immigration Reform and Control Act tackled the issue of illegal immigration. In addition to imposing penalties on employers who hired undocumented workers, the act allowed illegal aliens and undocumented agricultural workers who had lived in the United States since 1981 to become citizens. Under this amnesty program, about 3.2 million illegal aliens received legal status. The 1986 act, however, failed to cut off the flow of undocumented workers into the economy. On the contrary, illegal aliens in many areas have had little difficulty obtaining false documents to qualify for jobs.

In 1990, Congress addressed the question of general immigration law for the first time since 1965. The Immigration Act of 1990 raised the limit on annual admissions to 675,000 immigrants. (The 1965 act had set the ceiling at 290,000.) The 1990 law also nearly tripled the number of immigration slots reserved for newcomers with prized job skills and their families. Based

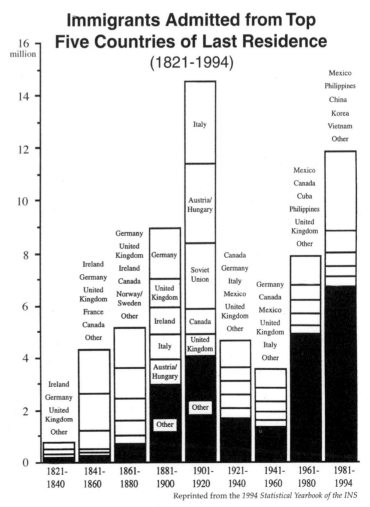

Immigrants Admitted from Top Five Countries of Last Residence (1821-1994)

Reprinted from the *1994 Statistical Yearbook of the INS*

Immigration to the U.S. in 1996
Relatives of U.S. citizens and permanent residents..................... 596,000
Skilled workers and their families.........117,000
Refugees...119,000
Asylees... 10,000
Miscellaneous.. 74,000
Illegal aliens (estimate)........................ 300,000
Total... 1,216,000

on the Immigration Act of 1990, over 71 percent of immigration visas go to family members of U.S. citizens and permanent legal residents; about 21 percent are set aside for well-trained workers and their families; and about 8 percent are available for immigrants from countries that have received relatively few visas in previous years.

In the 1990s, the immigration debate has increasingly been infused with ethnic tension and political division. Among the most significant pieces of legislation to surface has been the Illegal Immigration Reform and Immigrant Responsibility Act. In its original form, the measure would have reduced overall annual immigration to 535,000 (including refugees and asylum seekers) and strengthened border control efforts. By the time the bill was signed into law in 1996, however, its focus had been narrowed to curbing illegal immigration. Under the act, procedures for deporting illegal aliens and rejecting asylum claims have been streamlined. Critics warn that the law places too much power in the hands of the INS and denies legitimate refugees a fair hearing.

The next round of immigration legislation may be influenced by the recommendations of the Commission on Immigration Reform. The commission, which was created under the 1990 Immigration Act to conduct a wide-ranging review of U.S. immigration policy, is due to issue its final report in the fall of 1997.

Illegal immigration gains attention

As reflected by Congress, the issue of illegal aliens (or undocumented immigrants) has assumed center stage in the U.S. immigration debate. Of the approximately 300,000 illegal aliens who settle permanently in the United States each year, the INS estimates that 41 percent of them arrive as tourists, students, or businessmen and then stay beyond the limitations of their visas. Thousands use false documents to slip past immigration officials at our country's airports. The public spotlight, however, has zeroed in mainly on those who enter the country by crossing the U.S.-Mexican border.

Illegal aliens and border control are relatively new concepts in the history of U.S. immigration. There was not even an attempt to monitor the borders until 1924. Until 1968, there were no official limits on immigration from countries in the Western Hemisphere.

Mexican workers, in particular, were a critical part of the labor force in the Southwest. They generally worked in agriculture during the growing season and then returned to their homes in Mexico. In 1942, the *bracero* program gave this arrangement official status, permitting the entry of 4 million to 5 million temporary agricultural workers. Even after the *bracero* program ended in 1964, large farms and low-wage industries continued to rely on Mexican workers. Meanwhile, Mexico's high rate of unemployment and wage levels that were one-tenth of American standards pushed more laborers across the border. In 1972, the INS caught about 500,000 illegal aliens crossing the border. That figure had increased to nearly 1.8 million by 1986.

The composition of the illegal alien population has changed markedly in the last two decades. More women and children are entering the country illegally and fewer than one-quarter work in agriculture. In addition, Mexicans make up a smaller proportion of illegal aliens than in the past. Increasingly, illegal aliens are arriving from Central America, the Caribbean, and Asia. International smuggling rings, for example, funnel an estimated 100,000 illegal immigrants from South Asia and China across the U.S.-Mexican border annually.

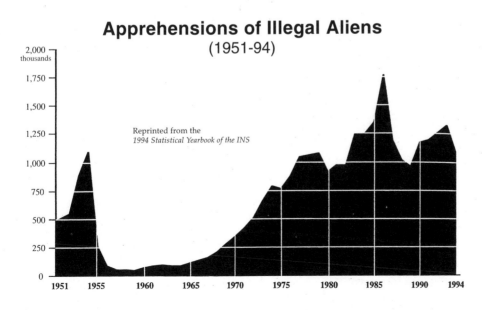

Apprehensions of Illegal Aliens
(1951-94)

Reprinted from the
1994 Statistical Yearbook of the INS

The U.S.-Mexican border near San Diego.

The increase in illegal immigration has prompted new approaches to border control. By 2001, the size of the INS's Border Patrol will be doubled, raising the total force to above 10,000. Border Patrol officials have also experimented with new strategies, such as concentrating their agents at the main crossing points. Nonetheless, the Border Patrol's task remains daunting. Outside of a handful of border cities, the 2,000-mile U.S.-Mexican frontier is marked either by the shallow Rio Grande or three strands of barbed wire.

Advocates of more stringent border control argue that the increased strength of the Border Patrol is crucial for national security. They point to studies showing that the U.S.-Mexican border is becoming a transit point for drug smuggling, and they fear that international terrorists may use the same route. The cost of providing social services to the more than 4 million illegal aliens in the United States is also part of the border control debate. Like immigrants in general, illegal aliens are concentrated in a few states, primarily California (which is home to about half of all undocumented immigrants), Texas, New York, Florida, and Illinois. In 1982, the Supreme Court ruled that states must provide illegal aliens with schooling. That decision, along with the growing proportion of women and children among the illegal alien population, has added to the education and health care budgets of several states. California, for instance, spends $1.8 billion annually on educating illegal immigrant children.

The same states that are burdened by the cost of social services for illegal aliens, however, also reap the rewards of their labor. Whether stitching pants in a clothing factory, washing dishes in a restaurant, or harvesting fruits and vegetables, illegal aliens are a crucial element of the work force in many areas. Critics of the practice maintain that some employers hire undocumented workers because they are unlikely to complain about low pay and poor working conditions.

Public concern over illegal immigration accounted for the passage of Proposition 187 by California voters in 1994. The ballot initiative was intended to deny illegal aliens in California schooling, welfare, non-emergency health care, and other social services, and would require administrators of government programs to report suspected illegal aliens to the INS. Opponents of Proposition 187, including President Bill Clinton, argued that the initiative is unconstitutional and would penalize the children of illegal immigrants most heavily. In addition, Mexican-American leaders complained that the proposition would heighten discrimination toward members of their ethnic group. Legal challenges have blocked implementation of Proposition 187 and are likely to keep the issue tied up in the courts for several years.

The passage of Proposition 187 and the 1996 Illegal Immigration Reform and Immigrant Responsibility Act has also had foreign policy repercussions. Mexican leaders warn that sealing off the border would revive anti-American feelings and hurt economic relations with the United States' third leading trading partner. U.S.-Mexican relations have taken on still greater importance since the enactment of the North American Free Trade Agreement (NAFTA) linking the economies of the United States, Mexico, and Canada. The agreement sets up a regional trading bloc of nearly 400 million people by lowering trade barriers among the three countries. Mexican officials and free trade advocates in the United States contend that by creating better-paying jobs in Mexico, NAFTA will reduce the flow of undocumented immigrants. Some experts on illegal immigration go further. They argue that by increasing foreign aid to Mexico and other Latin American countries and by encouraging low-wage American industries to invest in the region the United States can help generate new local jobs that will keep potential illegal aliens at home. Indeed, the turbulence of Mexico's economy has demonstrated the strong link between economic factors and illegal immigration. After the crash of the Mexican peso in late 1994, the Border Patrol recorded an upsurge in illegal crossings from Mexico.

Refugees in the foreign policy arena

In addition to illegal immigration, the issue of refugee policy has acquired greater prominence in recent years. The 1980 Refugee Act opened the United States to more refugees and changed the definition of refugee to conform to

Rob Rogers. Reprinted by permission of UFS, Inc.

United Nations (UN) standards. According to the 1980 act, a refugee is a person "unwilling or unable to return to such a country because of persecution or a well-founded fear of persecution on account of race, religion, nationality, membership in a particular social group, or political opinion."

U.S. refugee laws during the Cold War were primarily an instrument of foreign policy, with preference going to refugees escaping from communist countries. In the past two decades, however, a worldwide refugee crisis has challenged old assumptions. The internationally recognized refugee population has grown twelve times to 26 million, largely due to war and famine in the developing world, and refugee applications to the United States have shot up by more than twenty times.

U.S. policy, however, has been slow to change. Of the more than 1.2 million refugees admitted from 1981 to 1991, 94 percent came from communist nations. Even with the end of the Cold War, old foreign policy priorities have continued to define refugee admissions. Of the 128,600 refugees and asylees accepted in 1996, 29,700 traced their origins to Vietnam, 22,500 to Cuba, and 26,400 to either Ukraine or Russia.

Critics of U.S. refugee policy are sharply divided among themselves. Some charge that the United States has lost sight of humanitarian considerations in awarding immigration visas. They want refugee and asylum applicants to be evaluated in strict accordance with UN standards, regardless of the political significance of their countries of origin. Others assert that many of the people admitted as refugees and asylum seekers are not fleeing persecution but simply looking for a better life. They favor lowering the overall ceiling for refugees.

Caribbean "boat people"

Dual refugee crises in the Caribbean in 1994 spotlighted the clash of values and interests surrounding U.S. policy. Haitian refugees were the first to grab America's attention. Beginning in 1992, thousands of Haitians set sail for American shores after the United States imposed an economic embargo on Haiti to force the country's military leaders from power. Presidents George Bush and Bill Clinton both tried to discourage the outpouring of Haitian "boat people." Although a few were granted refugee status, the majority were turned back by the U.S. Coast Guard. By the summer of 1994, U.S. authorities were holding 14,000 Haitians at the U.S. naval base in Guantanamo Bay, Cuba. The refugee crisis was a key factor in Clinton's decision to send 20,000 troops to Haiti in September 1994 to spearhead an international mission to restore democratic government on the island.

Even as the events in Haiti unfolded, the United States was grappling with an influx of thousands of Cuban boat people. The backdrop of the Cuban crisis was very different from developments in Haiti. Since Fidel Castro's

Bettmann

Cuban refugees rowing toward the Florida coast in August 1994.

Turn-of-the-century immigrants approach New York.

first steps toward establishing a communist dictatorship in Cuba in 1959, the United States had readily accepted Cubans seeking refuge. In 1980, the United States took in 125,000 Cuban refugees, including hundreds of criminals released by Castro from Cuban prisons.

When Cuban authorities suddenly lifted restrictions on emigration in the summer of 1994, U.S. officials feared a repeat of the 1980 exodus. Tens of thousands of Cubans headed out to sea on flimsy vessels or even inner tubes. Unlike 1980, however, the United States denied the boat people automatic entry. Instead, the United States negotiated with Cuban officials — something U.S. leaders had long avoided — and worked out an agreement to normalize Cuban immigration to the United States. Under the accord, the United States pledged to accept 20,000 Cuban immigrants annually in exchange for Cuba's commitment to block illegal immigration.

The shift in policy toward Cuba removed a double standard in America's position on refugees. Critics had long charged that Cuban refugees received preferential treatment because they were fleeing a communist country. The U.S. policy of turning back Haitian boat people also sparked accusations of racism. Haitian President Jean-Bertrand Aristide, for example, claimed in 1994 that the United States was discriminating against his countrymen because they were black. Although U.S. officials have strongly rejected charges of racism, they have voiced concerns about attracting a flood of would-be immigrants from throughout the Caribbean Basin.

Doors closing abroad

The United States is not alone among developed countries wrestling with refugee problems. In Europe, the collapse of communism and the outbreak of civil wars in the former Soviet bloc triggered a flow of refugees westward. Germany has been on the front line of the crisis. From 1989 to 1992, Germany took in nearly 900,000 asylum seekers. In the summer of 1993, however, Germany tightened its definition of political asylum and began deporting foreigners who did not meet the new standards.

Other European countries quickly followed Germany's lead. France's interior minister went so far as to declare that France should move "toward zero immigration." Member states of the fifteen-nation European Union are considering the adoption of a single immigration policy for the entire trade bloc.

In Canada too, recent adjustments in immigration standards reflect a change in priorities. In 1996, Canada admitted 220,000 immigrants — a much higher percentage of its population compared to that of the United States. Unlike America's immigration laws, however, Canadian standards are geared toward admitting young, college-educated newcomers who speak fluent English or French. Emphasis on reunifying families has been downgraded.

SECTION 3

Views on U.S. options

Now that you have read about some of the issues related to U.S. immigration policy, it is time to take a closer look at what our country's position should be. In this section, you will explore four views on U.S. immigration policy. As you will see, each of the views is based on a distinct set of values and beliefs, and is shaped by a well-defined perspective on the threats and opportunities facing the United States.

The views presented address three fundamental questions that frame the discussion on U.S. immigration policy:

•**What should be the overall purpose of U.S. immigration policy?** Should our policy be driven by humanitarian concerns, such as reunifying families, responding to political persecution, and providing opportunity for people beyond our shores? Or should our policy be crafted to match U.S. economic needs by offering immigration visas mainly to highly skilled applicants and by introducing a guest worker program for low-wage industries?

•**What should be the message that America sends to people beyond our borders?** Should we be seen as a country that welcomes the energy, talent, and dynamism brought by immigrants from throughout the world? Or should we encourage would-be immigrants to stay home and, with our assistance, contribute to the development of their own societies?

•**How should we enforce U.S. immigration policy?** Should we tighten

169

control of our borders and take stronger steps to deport illegal aliens? Or should we avoid measures that may infringe on civil liberties or offend minority communities?

Each of the four views that follows responds differently to the above questions. You should think of the views as a tool designed to help you examine the contrasting strategies from which Americans must define our country's role in the world and craft future policy.

View 1 — *Opening ourselves to the world*

Americans can take pride in a heritage that promotes openness, tolerance, and diversity. Immigration is critical to America's vitality. Our national ethos fits the world that is emerging, where barriers to international understanding are falling, borders have less significance, and a new era of global interaction is dawning. Immigration puts our country in touch with the tastes and preferences of consumers worldwide, and gives U.S. companies an edge in opening export markets. Keeping our doors open lets the world know that the United States remains a country that looks forward to tomorrow.

Considering trade-offs

• Will continuing to open our doors to millions of mostly unskilled immigrants overtax our social service system and aggravate the problems of Americans at the bottom of the economic ladder?

• Will high levels of immigration push U.S. population past tolerable limits and inflict still more harm on our country's environment?

• Will the influx of large numbers of immigrants eventually overwhelm American culture and contribute to the fragmentation of our society?

View 2 — *Balancing our responsibilities*

To remain responsible citizens in today's changing world, we need a new policy on immigration. A multi-pronged approach makes the most sense. By improving life among our neighbors, we can get a grip on the forces that drive desperate immigrants toward our country's shores. If we are to effectively join other developed countries in addressing the problems that plague much of the developing world (such as environmental pollution, unsanitary living conditions, and the spread of disease), we must restore the health of our own society. The money we currently spend on settling immigrants should be directed domestically toward our own disadvantaged citizens and internationally in the form of foreign aid programs that promote responsible, long-term development in Mexico, the Caribbean, and other poor areas. Finally, consistent, humane standards for granting political asylum to refugees should be established.

Considering trade-offs

•Will new foreign aid programs fail to overcome the deep-seated problems in much of Latin America and the Caribbean, yet swell the U.S. budget deficit?

•Will closing our own doors to immigrants increase international tension, rather than improve global harmony?

•Will establishing a more open policy toward refugees encourage millions of desperate people to try to enter the United States?

View 3 — Competing in a competitive world

Although the Cold War is over, competition among nations has grown only more intense. We are still a growing country, with enormous resources and human potential, but we have let our competitive edge slip away in the past few decades. Our country requires an immigration policy that fits our overall economic needs. To spur American high-tech industries forward, our doors should be open to scientists and engineers from abroad. To help American factories, farms, and service industries hold down costs, we should allow a limited number of foreigners to work temporarily in low-wage jobs. By forging ahead with realistic choices, we can make our immigration policy work for us.

Considering trade-offs

•Will drawing the best and brightest skilled workers from poor countries undercut economic development in much of the world and damage U.S. foreign relations, especially with our neighbors to the south?

•Will reducing the number of immigration visas available for family reunification leave many close relatives apart?

•Will admitting foreigners as temporary workers create a group of second-class citizens with few rights and little stake in American society?

View 4 — Recognizing our limits

The world is changing at a breakneck pace. The population explosion in poor countries, the spread of war and chaos, and the age-old curses of hunger and disease plague an ever-growing portion of humanity. We must recognize that Americans can do little to end the misery that haunts much of the world. Simply maintaining our way of life amounts to a major challenge. Although the United States is a nation of immigrants, the arguments supporting massive immigration have long since passed into history. Now it is time to say enough. We should drastically reduce the number of immigrants we accept and commit the resources necessary to take control of our borders.

Considering trade-offs

• Will closing the door on new immigrants deprive the American work force of skills, talent, and ambition, and create a society that lacks a solid understanding of the world beyond our borders?

• Will efforts to crack down against illegal aliens make foreign-born Americans a target of suspicion and discrimination?

• Will fencing off our neighbors to the south spark anti-American feelings in Latin America and the Caribbean, and harm relations with many of our leading trading partners?

Your turn

These views are by no means the only U.S. options. Rather, they are intended to lay out some of the most important values and assumptions underlying the debate on U.S. immigration policy and to spur discussion on the direction our country should take regarding this pressing issue. When you meet next time, you will have an opportunity to discuss U.S. immigration policy with others. The following statements are designed to help you clarify your thoughts on what is most important to you concerning this issue. Take a few moments to respond. This is a tool for you to get started. It will not be collected.

Rate each of the statements according to your beliefs:

1 = Strongly Support	3 = Oppose	5 = Undecided
2 = Support	4 = Strongly Oppose	

___ International stability and order should be protected because they are vital to the interests of the United States.

___ As the most powerful nation in the world, the United States has a responsibility to address human suffering wherever it occurs.

___ Americans will face a struggle in the coming decades just to maintain their present lifestyle.

____ The United States must remain a symbol of hope and opportunity for the people of the world.

____ The United States should oppose countries that grossly abuse the human rights of their citizens.

____ Problems in the international arena are far less important for Americans than the challenges we face at home, such as poverty, crime, and budget deficits.

____ The United States should recognize that problems in the developing world, such as poverty and environmental degradation, must be addressed as problems that affect everyone on the planet.

____ In the end, U.S. foreign policy should be based on a realistic assessment of our national interest, not on idealistic plans for saving the world.

____ The greatness of the United States is based on its diversity and openness to fresh ideas.

_3_ The problems affecting most poor countries are only going to get worse, regardless of U.S. foreign aid programs.

Suggested reading

Mills, Nicolaus, ed. *Arguing Immigration: The Debate over the Changing Face of America* (New York: Simon and Schuster, 1994).

Portes, Alejandro. *City on the Edge: The Transformation of Miami* (Berkeley, California: University of California Press, 1993).

Schlesinger, Arthur M., Jr. *The Disuniting of America: Reflections on a Multicultural Society* (New York: W.W. Norton, 1992).

Ungar, Sanford J. *Fresh Blood: The New American Immigrants* (New York: Simon and Schuster, 1995).

Chapter 9

Charting Our Future: Balancing Priorities

When the heads of the world's leading industrial democracies convened in Denver in 1997, the occasion gave President Bill Clinton cause to celebrate a golden historical moment for the United States. As Clinton noted, a rare convergence of events has blessed the United States with an almost unprecedented combination of peace and prosperity.

Internationally, the United States stands tall as the world's sole superpower. No country rivals America's military might or diplomatic leverage. Moreover, there are no likely threats to America's supremacy looming on the horizon, at least not in the coming decade.

Economically, the United States is setting the pace in adapting to the demands of globalization. America enjoys a nearly ideal balance of steady growth, low unemployment, and restrained inflation. U.S. companies have mastered the technologies of tomorrow and restored America's competitive edge in critical industries. Our leaders can again put forth the United States as a model of dynamism, creativity, and efficiency.

Indeed, Americans have reason to take pride in our country's accomplishments. History has seldom been so generous. At the same time, we know from past experience that such times are fleeting. Only recently, our country was gripped by a pervasive sense of anxiety and malaise. Prudence tells us that we should take advantage of the current respite to plan for the future. Yet despite our better judgment, we as a nation have turned away from many of the issues warranting our attention.

In foreign affairs, Americans are oddly disengaged from the world that we dominate. Polls indicate that we are less interested in developments overseas than at any time since World War II. The public mood, however, cannot turn back the forces that are shrinking our planet. Advances in communication and transportation will continue to bring us into closer contact with our neighbors. The boom in international trade and investment will inevitably link us economically to a greater share of humanity. New global challenges posed by global warming, refugee crises, and deadly epidemics will require us to look beyond our borders with greater frequency. The rise of China, instability in the Middle East, Russia's uncertain transition, and a myriad of conflicts elsewhere will remind us of the security dangers we all face in the nuclear age.

At home, Americans are also vulnerable to the charge of complacency. For the moment, the federal budget deficit has been tamed, but our political leaders remain wary of tackling the long-term problems of social security, medicare, and other middle-class entitlements. The vigor of our economy has done little to bridge the gulf separating the haves and have-nots in our society. Rather, a growing portion of America's affluent are abandoning public institutions. Without the Cold War, universal military service, or the commitment fostered by the civil rights movement or other far-reaching national causes, we increasingly lack the civic glue to hold us together as a nation.

Years from now, Americans may look back on our present good fortune as a unique opportunity for addressing the nation's public policy agenda. We will likely be judged by our willingness to confront difficult problems, honestly evaluate trade-offs, and assess long-term consequences. In this final chapter, you will consider many of the questions that we as a nation have been reluctant to examine. Your responsibility is to think about how the United States should fit into the world that is emerging and define our country's international policy goals for the coming years.

At the concluding session of this series, you will have an opportunity to develop your own preferred Future. Your Future should not be a utopian blueprint, but a broad sketch of the direction that you believe the nation should head in the coming years. This is your Future, and as such it should represent your vision for our country's role in the world. You need not be constrained by what is politically viable today, because in a democracy it is the citizens together that define that will. The Future you propose should be possible if we have the will as a nation.

The following pages call on you to clarify the beliefs and sort out the priorities that will serve as the foundation for your Future.

Section 1

Focusing your thoughts

The statements in this section are designed to help you focus your thoughts about the issues facing us at this historic turning point. Take a few moments to respond. This is a tool to help you get started. It will not be collected.

Rate each of the statements according to your beliefs:

1 = Strongly Support   3 = Oppose   5 = Undecided

2 = Support   4 = Strongly Oppose

___ Involving ourselves in the affairs of other countries is wasteful and dangerous.

____ The United States should recognize that problems in the developing world, such as poverty and environmental degradation, must be addressed as problems that affect everyone on the planet.

____ U.S foreign policy should be directed toward promoting American values in other countries.

____ International stability and order should be protected because they are vital to the interests of the United States.

____ We should rely less on military force and other conventional foreign policy tools to solve the problems of today's interconnected world.

____ Questions of morality should not determine our relations with other countries.

____ The interests of the United States can be maintained only if we resolutely exercise our power and influence in international affairs.

____ As Americans, we have the right and the responsibility to spread democracy around the world.

____ Problems in the international arena are far less important for Americans than the challenges we face at home, such as poverty, crime, and budget deficits.

____ The United States should be willing to give up some of its own sovereignty to promote international cooperation.

____ The United States cannot afford to give other nations a say in policies by which Americans must live.

____ The United States should oppose countries that grossly abuse the human rights of their citizens.

SECTION 2

Weighing risks and trade-offs

Beliefs come with trade-offs. We may, for example, believe in peace, but we also must ask ourselves what we are willing to do in the name of peace.

Are we willing to turn a blind eye to egregious violations of human rights to avoid international confrontations? Are we willing to grant the United Nations new powers to slap down potential aggressors at the expense of our own sovereignty? Are we willing to scale back research on high-tech weaponry in hopes that other countries might follow a similar course?

Weighing risks and trade-offs is central to the formulation of public policy. The following section presents the possible implications of the beliefs in Section 1. As you reflect on the issues raised in this section, compare your responses to those you gave in Section 1. Feel free to revise your ratings based on your reflections. Your responses in Section 1 will provide a useful tool for you as you develop your own Future during the final session of this series.

Involving ourselves in the affairs of other countries is wasteful and dangerous.

> *Would you support this statement even if it means that...*

- shutting down U.S. foreign aid programs will increase human suffering in poor countries?

- nations hostile to our interests will fill the vacuum left by the United States in the Middle East and elsewhere?

- progress toward democracy and economic reform in the developing world will be reversed when U.S. programs end?

The United States should recognize that problems in the developing world, such as poverty and environmental degradation, must be addressed as problems that affect everyone on the planet.

> *Would you support this statement even if it means that...*

- the United States will be expected to provide large sums of money to support efforts to improve conditions in other countries?

- American relief workers and troops will be called upon to join in international efforts, often in countries far from home?

- additional U.S. aid will go toward propping up corrupt, incompetent leaders in the developing world?

179

U.S. foreign policy should be directed toward promoting American values in other countries.

Would you support this statement even if it means that...

• tension will escalate with countries that reject our values?

• new divisions will arise within the international community centered on questions of values?

• anti-Western forces, such as Islamic fundamentalism, will gain greater prominence in cultures that do not share our values?

International stability and order should be protected because they are vital to the interests of the United States.

Would you support this statement even if it means that...

• we must always defend the international status quo, regardless of its fairness and legitimacy?

• we will have to respond to every threat to international order and stability?

• we will be expected to aid governments that are fighting insurgents within their countries, regardless of the reasons for civil conflict?

We should rely less on military force and other conventional foreign policy tools to solve the problems of today's interconnected world.

Would you support this statement even if it means that...

• regional aggressors will be convinced that the United States will not block their efforts to expand their influence by force?

• global problems will remain unresolved because the United States lacks clout in the international arena?

• the international system that has evolved in the 20th century will grow increasingly fragmented and chaotic?

Questions of morality should not determine our relations with other countries.

Would you support this statement even if it means that...

• international bullies will increase their aggression against their neighbors, knowing that there is no one to stop them?

- ethnic cleansing and genocide will become more widespread in the developing world and the former Soviet bloc?

- the emerging consensus in the international community on questions of human rights will dissolve?

The interests of the United States can be maintained only if we resolutely exercise our power and influence in international affairs.

Would you support this statement even if it means that...

- we must use military force and risk American lives for less than admirable causes?

- we will anger our allies and trading partners by acting independently?

- we must maintain high military spending to deter our potential enemies?

As Americans, we have the right and the responsibility to spread democracy around the world.

Would you support this statement even if it means that...

- other countries will resent our active promotion of democracy?

- laying the groundwork for democracy will require expensive new foreign aid programs?

- we must send American troops far from home to defend democratic governments under attack?

Problems in the international arena are far less important for Americans than the challenges we face at home, such as poverty, crime, and budget deficits.

Would you support this statement even if it means that...

- we will sit on the sidelines as the next Adolf Hitler gains strength?

- global problems, such as degradation of the environment, AIDS, and drug trafficking, will worsen?

- the international alliance system will break down, endangering world peace?

The United States should be willing to give up some of its own sovereignty to promote international cooperation.

Would you support this statement even if it means that...

- the United States will be obliged to live by the decisions of the UN and other international bodies even when they run counter to U.S. interests?

- American taxpayers will have to support expensive new programs and powerful bureaucracies created by the international community?

- the United States will be able to take military action only with the approval of the UN?

The United States cannot afford to give other nations a say in policies by which Americans must live.

Would you support this statement even if it means that...

- the United States will find itself isolated in the international arena?

- the UN, the international trading system, and other global institutions will unravel without U.S. participation?

- other great powers, such as China or Russia, will emerge as leaders in the international community?

The United States should oppose countries that grossly abuse the human rights of their citizens.

Would you support this statement even if it means that...

- we will anger some of our key trading partners and military allies, especially in the Middle East?

- we will aggravate tensions with other great powers, such as China and Russia?

- the cohesion and effectiveness of the UN and other international organizations will be undermined?

Having completed this section, please take a moment to review your ratings in Section 1. Did you change them?

Crafting your future

When you meet for the final session of this series, you will have the opportunity to articulate your own vision for the United States during the next decade. You will need to ask yourself what is most important to you. Perhaps you have found that some of the things you care deeply about are in conflict. What consequences are unacceptable? What trade-offs are you willing to make? Use your responses to the questions in this chapter to help you frame your own Future. For example, statements in Section 1 to which you have assigned "1" or "2" can serve as points that you may want to include. Those to which you have assigned "3" or "4" you may want to include in their negative form. You may also wish to incorporate your responses to the *"Your Turn"* sections from previous chapters. As you synthesize the various elements to frame a coherent vision of your Future, you might ask yourself these questions:

- What do you believe are the most important international problems facing the United States?
- How should we respond to the changes in the international environment to make the United States the country you believe it can and should be?
- How will these steps affect the lives of Americans over the next ten years?
- What would people who oppose this vision say?
- How would you respond to these people?
- At the turn of the century, what would we be able to say America stands for if your Future were adopted?

We hope that you will use the last session of this series not only to define your own Future, but also to share that vision with others and to explore areas in which you may share common ground. Finally, this session offers an opportunity for you to consider what you can do after this series ends to further your goals. In crafting your Future and participating in the ballot at the end of this book, you will be joining others in a national conversation about who we are as a nation and where we are headed as the next century approaches.